Berlitz®

G000109423

MUNICH

- A in the text denotes a highly recommended sight
- A complete A–Z of practical information starts on p.115
- Extensive mapping on cover flaps

Printed in Switzerland by Weber SA, Bienne.

1st edition (1995/1996)

**Although we make every effort to ensure the accuracy of the
information in this guide, changes do occur. If you have any new
information, suggestions or corrections to contribute to the guide,
we would like to hear from you. Please write to Berlitz Publishing
at the above address.**

Original text:	Jack Altman
Additional text:	Keith Strandberg, Clare Haigh
Editor:	Hazel Clarke
Photography:	Chris Coe; pp. 32, 86, 98 Eric Jaquier
Layout:	Suzanna Boyle
Cartography:	Falk-Verlag, Hamburg
Thanks to:	Eva Maria Nopper and the Munich Tourist Office for all their invaluable help.

Cover photographs: *Lenbachhaus*
back: *Musician on Odeonsplatz*

CONTENTS

The City and the People

To northerners seeking the easy, relaxed life of southern Europe, Munich seems almost Mediterranean. This last main stop before the Alps provides, for many, a first breath of Italy.

By the same token, southern Europeans travelling towards the prosperous efficiency of the cooler north find the cultural transition less abrupt if they go by way of Munich, the Bavarian capital – a city which is more Baroque than Gothic and more green than gray. In fact, many southern Europeans – Greeks, Czechs, Italians – decide quite simply to stop in Munich and enjoy the best of both worlds – to Munich's advantage. Today, even the Italians themselves claim the city has the best Italian restaurants north of the Alps.

For Munich's genius has always been its ability to combine the Germanic talent for getting things done with a specifically Bavarian need to do them pleasantly. Business lunches seem to last a little longer here, and office hours seem to be a little shorter. Yet no one who has witnessed the city's impressive affluence, its dynamic car industry, brilliantly constructed Olympic sports complex and splendid underground system would suggest that this delightfully relaxed attitude was unproductive.

If the people of Munich do differ so much from other Germans, that is because, you'll be told, this isn't Germany, it's Bavaria. As the capital of the fervently Catholic and conservative Free State of Bavaria, Munich epitomizes the independent Bavarian spirit. Here, good-natured local chauvinism knows no bounds – whole books are crammed with jokes about stiff-necked Prussians. At the city's renowned Oktoberfest, the annual beer festival, visitors sing 'Warum ist es am Rhein so schön?' (Why is it so lovely on the Rhine?) to the great amusement of the locals who, they say, don't have to ask themselves why Bavaria is so lovely.

View of the Neues Rathaus and the rooftops of Munich from the tower of St Peter's Church.

The Oktoberfest is, perhaps, what first strikes the popular imagination in relation to Munich. Indeed, with annual consumption of 7,000,000 litres of beer by 8,000,000 visitors – including more than one million children – it is a grandiose event, quite appropriate to the oversized image the Bavarians have of their capital. It is also the most extravagant expression of that untranslatable feeling of warm fellowship known in German as *Gemütlichkeit*.

But it would be wrong to think of life in Munich merely as one long Oktoberfest. As a result of the post-war division of Berlin, Munich became the undisputed cultural capital of the Federal Republic of Germany – no mean achievement, in the face of the considerable claims of Hamburg, Frankfurt and Cologne. The opera house and concert halls make the town a musical mecca still, especially for the performance of works by Mozart, Wagner and Richard Strauss.

Painters also appreciate the favourable artistic climate of the city, particularly in the bohemian district of Schwabing, which exploded onto the international scene in the 20th century as a centre for the Blaue Reiter school, which included Wassily Kandinsky, Paul Klee and Franz Marc. Munich still has some of the world's most innovative galleries, as well as the superbly displayed classical and modern collections of the Alte and Neue Pinakothek museums, both of which are richly endowed.

Munich has become a centre for industry and publishing, and also for the much-admired New German Cinema and its world-famous directors, Volker Schloendorff, Werner Herzog and Edgar Reitz.

But there is also a darker side to the city – Adolf Hitler's early association with Munich and the formation there of the Nazi Party – with all the ugliness that this entailed for the social and architectural identity of Bavaria's capital. Yet it was Munich's cultural atmosphere that originally attracted the future dictator to the city, at a time when he still dreamed of becoming a great painter. The stormy years from 1918 to 1945 were, in the end, a brief political interlude for Munich, and its people seem happy to

A city rich in history, art and culture, Munich has some of the country's best art galleries.

have relinquished the political spotlight to Bonn and Berlin.

Munich has tried, however, to retain its historical identity. After the destruction resulting from World War II, many German cities decided to break with the past and rebuild in a completely modern style. But the Bavarian capital preferred to painstakingly restore and reconstruct the great churches and palaces of its past. There are plenty of modern skyscrapers, but the heart of the old city has authentically recaptured its Baroque charm. Some people thought that the reconstruction and renovation were too thorough, too 'clean', but, a few decades later, the ravages of pollution have given the new-old buildings a patina of age that it used to take centuries to acquire. In fact, because the city's reconstruction has been so complete and so convincing, monuments such as the Siegestor (Victory Gate) have been left in their bomb-scarred condition as a historic token.

The inner city is a pedestrian's delight, thanks both to a clever road system that keeps the majority of the traffic circling the city centre rather than crossing through it (except by means of underpasses) and to an excellent system of public transport. Beyond the city centre the broad, tree-lined avenues and boulevards planned by Bavaria's last kings open up the town and provide a considerable touch of elegance.

The Englischer Garten, immensely enhanced by the ebullient River Isar, is a veritable jewel among Europe's great parks. The river's swiftly flowing waters are evidence of the proximity of the Alps, where the river has its source. On a clear day, the mountains seem to lie just beyond the city's southern suburbs. That's when the *Föhn* is blowing: the famous wind that gives some a headache and inspires others with phenomenally clear creative insights – a characteristic Munich ambiguity.

When the mountains reappear on the city's doorstep, they remind the people of the countryside from which many of them, or their parents, first came. Every weekend there is a massive exodus to the surrounding villages and lakes: east to the Chiemsee; west and south to the Ammersee, Starnberger See and Tegernsee; and northward to Schleissheim and Freising. Here the citizens of Munich can indulge in hiking, sailing, hunting and fishing – or visiting aunts and uncles for coffee and cakes.

In the winter, they trek further south into the mountains for skiing, an integral part of Munich life. Although Munich is undoubtedly a metropolis, and in many ways a sophisticated one, the city also retains a resolutely rural atmosphere, never losing sight of its origins in the peasant hinterland. Visitors would be wrong not to participate in Munich's happy mixture of town and country.

Shaded beer gardens offer plenty of opportunity for sampling the local specialities.

A Brief History

Munich was a late arrival on the Bavarian scene. During the Middle Ages, at a time when Nuremberg, Augsburg and Regensburg were already thriving cities, the present-day state capital was just a small settlement housing a few peasants and some Benedictine monks from Lake Tegern. The site was known in the eighth century quite simply as *Ze den Munichen*, a dialect form of *zu den Mönchen* (the monks' place). Accordingly, Munich's coat of arms today bears the image of a child in a monk's habit, the Münchner Kindl.

In 1156, the settlement of the River Isar attracted the attention of Heinrich der Löwe (Henry the Lion), the Duke of Saxony and Bavaria, who was cousin of the German Emperor Frederick Barbarossa. He was looking for a place to set up a toll station for the passage of salt, a lucrative product from nearby Salzburg. Until then, tolls had been collected by the powerful bishop of Freising at

Oberföhring Bridge, just to the north. Duke Heinrich burned this bridge down, and built a new one, together with a market, customs house and mint, at a fork in the Isar.

Bishop Otto of Freising was himself an uncle of Frederick Barbarossa, and protested to the emperor, who decided to leave Munich in Heinrich's hands, but to grant one-third of the toll revenues to the diocese of Freising – dues that were paid until 1852. The day of the emperor's decision, 14 June 1158, is recognized as the date of Munich's founding.

The salt trade made Munich prosperous and the settlement grew rapidly into a town. In 1180, after Heinrich refused military aid for the emperor's foreign wars, Frederick Barbarossa threatened to raze Munich to the ground. However, Bishop Otto pleaded the city's case, as he was making a great deal of money from his share of the salt duty. Munich was saved, but the city was handed over to the Wittelsbach family, who ruled Bavaria for the next seven centuries.

HISTORICAL LANDMARKS

8th century	Small settlement of Benedictine monks gives the site its name, *Ze den Munichen*.
1158	Henry the Lion sets up toll station for the passage of salt from Salzburg.
1180	Emperor Barbarossa takes Munich from Henry and hands city over to the Wittelsbach family.
1328	Duke Ludwig IV becomes Holy Roman Emperor – court established in Munich.
1348	Black Death brings devastation to Munich.
15th century	Prosperous period – Munich established as transit point for trade from Venice.
1632	Swedish armies invade Munich during the Thirty Years' War; Munich devastated by plague.
1638	Mariensäule set up on Marienplatz.
1704-1714	Austrian occupation of Munich.
1742	Hungarian hussars take over the city.
1789	American Benjamin Thompson develops today's Englischer Garten as a public park.
1805	Napoleon visits Munich.
1806	Napoleon raises Bavaria to status of Kingdom.
1845	Bavarian King Ludwig II is born.
1886	Ludwig II found drowned at Schloss Berg.
1918	The Bavarian Republic declared. Ludwig III flees.
1920	Adolph Hitler addresses the Deutsche Arbeiter-Partei at the Hofbräuhaus.
1923	Hitler stages his famous 'Beer Hall Putsch'.
1935	Munich named Capital of the Nazi Movement.
1939-1945	World War II, 71 air raids on the city, killing 6,000 and wounding 16,000.
1972	Munich hosts the Summer Olympic Games.
1985	Opening of the Gasteig Philharmonic.
1992	Opening of the new airport, Flughafen München Franz Josef Strauss.

The Wittelsbachs Take Over

By the end of the 13th century, Munich was the largest town in the Wittelsbach dominions. However, the prosperous Munich burghers grew discontented and began to press Duke Ludwig the Stern (1229-94) for a larger piece of the pie. In defence, the duke built himself

The Angel of Peace watches over the river Isar and the gardens of the Prinzregententerrasse.

a fortress, the Alter Hof, parts of which can still be seen just west of the Hofbräuhaus.

Munich entered the international political arena in 1328, when Duke Ludwig IV (1294-1347) was made Holy Roman Emperor. With his court firmly established in Munich, he enlisted scholars from all over Europe as his advisors. Perhaps the most notable of these were Marsiglio of Padua and William of Occam, philosophers who defended secular power against that of the Pope and thus made themselves useful allies for Ludwig. William of Occam became famous for 'Occam's Razor', in which he states, roughly, that if you've found a simple explanation for a problem, don't look for a complicated one. The Bavarians like that kind of thinking.

Troubled Times

The Black Death brought devastation to Munich in 1348. The city suffered social unrest, abrupt economic decline and the debasement of its currency. In a mass psychotic reaction to the catastrophe, citizens went on a wild rampage, massacring Jews for alleged ritual murder.

High taxes and widespread penury caused the burghers to revolt against the patricians. In 1385, the people took a cloth merchant, Hans Impler, from his house to the Schrannenplatz (now Marienplatz) and beheaded him. The patricians and their princes demanded draconian financial compensation and the situation deteriorated into open rebellion from 1397 to 1403.

By bringing in heavy military reinforcements, the Wittelsbachs regained the upper hand without being forced to make any of the far-reaching civic concessions won by the guilds of other German towns, such as Augsburg, Hamburg and Cologne. To secure their position during these troubled times, the Wittelsbachs built a sturdy Residenz on what was then the north-west corner of town. The massive, fortress-like palace (see p.40) attests to the level of protection needed to keep this despotic monarchy safe from its own people.

Reform and Counter-Reform

Dissent eased in the 15th century and trade boomed in salt, wine and cloth. The town also served as a transit point for the rich 'Venice goods' of spices and gold. During this period of renewed prosperity were built the great Frauenkirche, still a town symbol, as well as the Gothic civic citadel of the Altes Rathaus.

By the middle of the 16th century, an architectural rivalry had grown up between the burghers – who favoured the German Gothic style for their homes, and the Bavarian nobles – who preferred the Renaissance styles of Spain and Italy. The appearance of Munich in the 1500s is preserved in Jakob Sandtner's city model on display in the Bavarian National Museum (see p.63). However, most of the original buildings were later replaced by the Baroque and Rococo palaces of the 17th and 18th centuries and the neo-Gothic and neo-Classical buildings of the Industrial Revolution.

The Bavarian aristocracy's preference for foreign styles was in many ways a reaction to the subversive implications of German nationalism which had grown out of the Reformation. In 1510, when Martin Luther passed through Munich on his way to Rome, his still relatively orthodox preaching met with sympathy. But, some ten years later, Luther's revolutionary position aroused the anger of the traditionally conservative Bavarians, and Duke Wilhelm IV introduced the severe measures advocated by the Jesuits. Rebellious monks and priests were arrested and executed. In 1527, the repression culminated in the drowning or burning of 29 members of Munich's Baptist community who refused to recant.

The religious conflict concealed a competition for political and economic power. The city's bourgeoisie had seen in the Reformation an opportunity to push for the social reforms which the aristocracy had adamantly resisted. In the struggles that followed, the burghers were forced to relinquish the salt monopoly to the administration of the state.

With a certain vindictiveness, the nobles flaunted their political triumph with sumptuous festivities at court, such as those arranged to pay homage to Emperor Charles V and his Spanish retinue during their Munich visit of 1530. The climax of such pomp and circumstance in grand Renaissance style was the three-week-long wedding celebrations of Duke Wilhelm V and his bride, Renata of Lorraine, in 1568.

The patricians received spiritual support from the Jesuits, who were brought to Munich by Duke Wilhelm V to establish a school and to set up a theatre for the performance of morality plays. Some people resented this foreign influence, laying the foundation for the now perennial Bavarian distrust of outsiders.

Good Money After Bad

Such extravagant expenditure meant that the state coffers were empty by the time Maximilian I (1573-1651) came to

14

*M*arienplatz, once the site of the wheat market, and the heart of old Munich.

the throne. Even though the Bavarian state was now almost completely bankrupt, Maximilian (who was made Prince Elector in 1623) proceeded to build up a magnificent collection of art works. However painful this may have been for his tax-crippled subjects, we can be thankful to Maximilian for having thus laid the foundations of the Alte Pinakothek.

It was also Maximilian who ordered the splendid decorations that embellish the Residenz. Gustavus Adolphus of Sweden, who invaded Munich in 1632, during the cruel Thirty Years' War, was so impressed with the Residenz that he said he would have liked to carry the whole thing back to Stockholm on wheels. Instead, he settled for 42 Munich citizens, who were taken hostage against payment by Bavaria of 300,000 *Thaler* in war repara-

tions. (All but six of them returned three years later.)

In the Thirty Years' War (1618-48), bombardment damage was less in Munich than in many other German towns. However, starvation and disease wrought more havoc than the cannon. In 1634 the Black Death struck, taking a toll of 7,000 inhabitants, one-third of the city's population. In 1638, Maximilian set up the Mariensäule (Column of the Virgin Mary) as thanks for the town's deliverance from suffering.

Munich's Prince Electors frequently involved the city in **15** costly foreign adventures, thus rubbing salt into the wounds of civic poverty. In 1683, Max II Emanuel decided to help the Austrians beat off the Turks besieging Vienna. He promptly set out for Belgrade, and returned bringing 296 Turks as sedan-chair bearers and road-builders – Munich's first *Gastarbeiter* (immigrant workers). The Turkish Wars are commemorated in huge paintings that are on display in Schleissheim Castle. The city's debt as a result of the war totalled 20 million guilders.

During the War of the Spanish Succession (1701-14) Max Emanuel fought on the losing side, with the French, and Munich had to bear the burden of the Austrian occupation from 1704 to 1714. When the farmers rebelled, the ringleaders were arrested and hung, drawn and quartered on Marienplatz. Their heads were displayed on pikes at Isar Gate.

After the war, the Bavarian aristocracy was not especially sympathetic to the tribulations of the citizenry. The nobles set about building splendid little palaces for themselves, including the Preysing, the Erzbischöfliches (Archbishop's) and the Törring-Jettenbach Palais (now the General Post Office), strategically situated near the Prince Elector's Residenz.

*B*uilt by the Wittelsbachs as a defensive fortress, the opulent Residenz is now a museum.

Peace in an English Garden

The people of Munich grew ever more xenophobic after Hungarian hussars took over the city in 1742. They were dispatched by Empress Maria Theresa in retaliation for the Bavarian Prince Elector's opposition to Austro-Hungarian involvement in Germany.

In this atmosphere of hostility, Maximilian III Joseph (1727-77) could not have been surprised when the Munich bourgeoisie resisted his efforts to establish a court monopoly on the manufacture of goods. All the royal manufacturers went bankrupt, with the exception of Nymphenburg porcelain, which is still thriving to this day. A brighter note was struck with the building of the delightful Cuvilliéstheater and the performance there by one Wolfgang Amadeus Mozart of his operas *The Abduction from the Seraglio, The Marriage of Figaro* and *The Magic Flute.*

Maximilian III Joseph died in 1777, the last of the true Wittelsbach line, and the succession fell to Karl Theodor, a member of the Mannheim branch of the family. He didn't want to leave Mannheim, he didn't like Munich and Munich didn't like him. The people were starving; there was no bread; but, instead of wheat, Karl Theodor sent in soldiers to supress the angry populace.

It was Benjamin Thompson, an American, who suggested a solution to Karl Theodor's predicament. With the prince's blessing, Count Rumford – as he was subsequently known – provided schools and work to keep the unruly soldiers off the streets. He set up workshops and soup kitchens for the poor. (The potato-and-barley soup that was dispensed in them is served in Munich to this day, and known as *Rumfordsuppe.*)

In 1789, Rumford requisitioned a marshy wilderness on the outskirts of town and detailed the soldiers to drain it for development as a gigantic public park. The final result of Rumford's efforts, the Englischer Garten, is an enduring monument to American enterprise and know-how. **17**

New Hopes, Ancient Dreams

While Munich was cultivating its garden, the rest of Europe was in a revolutionary uproar. In such circumstances, the city could not remain isolated for long. In 1800, it was occupied by the French troops of General Jean Victor Moreau, who established his headquarters in Nymphenburg Palace.

*P*layground for the people of Munich since 1793, the Englischer Garten is a joy for picknickers.

Napoleon himself came to town in 1805 for the marriage of his wife Josephine's son, Eugène de Beauharnais, to Princess Augusta of Bavaria. The journey to Munich did not inconvenience the emperor too much, as it was on the way to Austerlitz, where he was to fight the Russians and Austrians. Napoleon elevated Max IV Joseph from Prince Elector to King of Bavaria, and in exchange took a vast contingent of Bavarians on his Russian campaign of 1812, where he left 30,000 of them to die on the battlefield. Under pressure from the French, Max Joseph emancipated the Protestants of Munich, improved conditions for the Jews and introduced a more moderate constitution.

Somehow, amid all the troubles of war and revolution, Munich managed to celebrate once again. Heeding the new spirit of the times, the royal court chose not to exclude the populace from the celebrations in honour of the marriage of Max Joseph's son, Ludwig, to Theresa of Saxony. On 17 October 1810, horse races were organized, with great success. They developed into an annual event – now the Oktoberfest.

Munich itself was gradually expanding to the north and west into Maxvorstadt, a region which links the city centre to Schwabing. The Graeco-Roman architecture of the Nationaltheater brought to the city the first signs of the classical spirit that was to become the obsession of Ludwig I.

Born in Strasbourg, Ludwig (1786-1868) was determined to break the French stranglehold on German culture and to make Munich a spearhead for a new nationalist movement.

During the Napoleonic occupation, the civic symbol of the Münchner Kindl had been replaced with an imperial lion; Ludwig made sure that the little monk was restored.

Familiar with the architecture of Rome and the Greek monuments of Sicily, Ludwig wanted to turn Munich into an 'Athens-on-the-Isar'. His first step was to move Bavaria's university from Landshut to Munich, where it was established along Ludwigstrasse in the Schwabing area first developed under his father's rule. **19**

He built majestic Odeonsplatz with its *Siegestor* (Gate of Victory). The gate, which was badly scarred by bombs during World War II, has since become a symbol of defeat. Königsplatz, with its Greek Revival architecture, was the most complete realization of Ludwig's classical aspirations. Typically, Ludwig himself laid the foundation stone for the Alte Pinakothek (the gallery designed to house the royal art collections) on 7 April 1826, the anniversary of the painter Raphael's birth.

A prodigious worker, rising before dawn each day to go to his office in the Residenz, the king gained some diversion from his sober duties by commissioning a series of portraits of the most beautiful young women of Munich. The collection hangs in the Schönheitengalerie (Gallery of Beautiful Women) at the Nymphenburg Palace. Included is his mistress, a dancer known as Lola Móntez, with whom he fell in love when he was 60 and she 28. She was Ludwig's ruin. He made her the Countess von Landsfeld, to the horror both of his conservative ministers and the radical university students. In 1848, as revolution swept Europe, the students and the angry citizens of Munich forced Ludwig to deport Lola, and he abdicated in disgust.

Ludwig I of Bavaria, who laid the foundation for some of the city's greatest institutions.

Ludwig's successor, Maximilian II (1811-64), boosted Munich's cultural reputation thanks to his intimacy with illustrious thinkers such as the historian Leopold von Ranke, the philosopher Friedrich von Schelling and the chemist Justus von Liebig.

End of a Dream

The last great king of Bavaria was the romantic king, Ludwig II (1845-86), famous for his collaboration with Richard Wagner. Under Ludwig's patronage, the composer staged in Munich the premières of his operas *Tristan and Isolde*, *The Mastersingers of Nuremberg*, *Rhinegold*, and *Valkyrie*.

In the mundane world of 19th-century industrial expansion, Ludwig dreamt of making Munich the music capital of the world. He wanted to build a gigantic theatre for his idol Wagner, a place where the composer could develop his concept of *Gesamtkunstwerk* – a synthesis of music, lyrics and theatre. But the banalities of state finances interfered and he was forced to relinquish the project to Bayreuth.

Ludwig acted out his fantasies in the eccentric fairy-tale palaces he built outside Munich – a medieval castle at Neuschwanstein, a beautiful French château at Linderhof, and a fanciful version of Versailles' Grand Trianon at Herrenchiemsee. Ironically, it was at a castle – the 16th-century Schloss Berg on Lake Starnberg – that Ludwig's life came to a sad and mysterious end.

By 1886, Ludwig's wild behaviour had persuaded the Bavarian government that he was mad, and a special commission declared him to be so. In consequence, the director of a mental asylum accompanied him to Schloss Berg and the two were later found drowned. It has never been determined whether their deaths were the result of murder or suicide.

Uncle Luitpold took over as regent (in place of Ludwig's brother, the insane King Otto). He presided over the grand *fin de siècle* artistic movement of the Jugendstil. This was followed a generation later by the **21**

The Residenz, home to the Wittelsbach dynasty for nearly five hundred years, until the eruption of World War I.

Blaue Reiter school which included Kandinsky, Klee and Marc. Thomas Mann, Rilke, Stefan George and other writers moved to Schwabing. The artistic ferment also attracted a young painter from Vienna, an embittered young man named Adolf Hitler.

The Wittelsbach dynasty, along with others in Vienna and Berlin, ended in the disaster of World War I. Bavarians resented having been dragged into the European conflict by what they felt was Prussian belligerence, and a new social democratic movement gained support. In November 1918, with the war in its last days, Kurt Eisner led a march of workers and peasants from the Theresienwiese. En route, disaffected soldiers took control of their barracks and hoisted the red flag of revolution.

In the Mathäser Bräuhaus – breweries traditionally being a favoured spot for political action in Munich – the Bavarian Republic was declared. The people invaded the Residenz and wandered around hooting for echoes in the vast galleries and ballrooms. Ludwig III, the last Wittelsbach king, fled in a car from the palace.

But the newly-born republic of workers, peasants and soldiers, modeled on the soviets created under the Russian revolution, was subject to violent attack from the conservative press and from private armies of troops (*Freikorps*) roaming the streets. Playing on Bavarian xenophobia, the right wing attacked Eisner as a Berliner and as a Jew. Just three months after the November revolution, Eisner was dead – shot down by a young aristocrat hoping to curry favour with an extreme right-wing club.

A group of 'coffee-house anarchists' led by the writers Ernst Toller and Erich Mühsam took over briefly, but they were soon replaced by hardline communists. After fierce and bloody fighting with the Freikorps, the Bavarian Red Army was defeated, and the short-lived independent republic of Bavaria was crushed.

In the space of six months, Munich had known in breathtaking succession a monarchy, revolutionary socialism, moderate socialism, anarchy, communism and, finally, brutal counter-revolutionary oppression. Thus, a tolerant tradition was swept away and the city became a breeding ground for extremist political and paramilitary groups.

Hitler's Munich

Adolf Hitler had first been drawn to Munich by its cultural ambiance, but he remained immune to the innovative tendencies of the avant-garde. His own painting was stolidly academic and attracted no attention. He turned to the clamour of German nationalism, and a chance photograph taken at a rally on Odeonsplatz in August 1914 shows Hitler in the crowd, joyfully greeting news of the declaration of war. **23**

He returned to Munich as a corporal in 1918. It was while working to re-educate soldiers in nationalistic, anti-Marxist ideas at the end of the Bavarian republic that he joined the Deutsche Arbeiter-Partei. By February 1920, he was able to address 2,000 members in the Hofbräuhaus. The association soon became known as the Nationalsozialistische Deutsche Arbeiter-Partei, or Nazi Party, and its symbol was the swastika. Armed storm troops of the party's Sturm-Abteilung (SA) broke up any opposition political meetings held in Munich.

At a January 1923 meeting Hitler said: 'Either the Nazi Party is the German movement of the future, in which case no devil can stop it, or it isn't, in which case it deserves to be destroyed.' Both proved true. By November, the party had 55,000 members and 15,000 storm troops. Hitler then felt strong enough to stage his famous Beer Hall Putsch.

Beer, Bluff and Bullets

The Beer Hall Putsch, which launched Hitler's national career, was staged in the Bürgerbräukeller. It gave a foretaste of the crazy melodrama, bluff and shameless gall he was later to exhibit on the world scene.

With the Bavarian minister Gustav von Kahr about to speak, Hitler burst into the crowded room, smashed a beer mug to the floor and pushed forward at the head of his storm troops, brandishing a pistol. In the pandemonium, he jumped on a table and fired a shot into the ceiling. 'National revolution has broken out!', he yelled. 'Farce! South America!' was the response from a few wags, who were promptly beaten up. The new Hitler-style of politics had indisputably arrived.

Today the Bürgerbräukeller has been replaced by the Hilton City Hotel – there is no plaque commemorating the putsch.

This was intended as a first move in the campaign to force the Bavarian state government to cooperate in a Nazi march on Berlin. The putsch ended in a debacle on Odeonsplatz and Hitler was sent to prison, but not before he had turned the whole affair to his advantage.

Hitler ensured that his trial for treason became an indictment of his prosecutors as accomplices of the 'November criminals', who, he said, had stabbed Germany in the back in 1918 with their anti-war movement. He became an instant hero. In prison at nearby Landsberg, Hitler was treated as an honoured guest. He was not required to perform prison work, but instead held political meetings and used his time to write *Mein Kampf*.

Hitler's career took him to Berlin, but the Nazis kept their party headquarters in Munich at the Brown House (named after the colour of their shirts). Brighter spirits of the time, including whimsical comedian Karl Valentin and a fan of his, dramatist Bertolt Brecht, also made their home in Munich.

*B*uilt for the 1972 Games, the Olympic Stadium provides impressive sports facilities.

In 1935, Munich became known as the 'Capital of the (Nazi) Movement'. Its status at the vanguard was confirmed in June 1938, when the central synagogue was looted, presaging the *Kristallnacht* (Crystal Night) rampage five months later, when most of Germany's Jewish shops and houses of prayer were destroyed.

In September of that year, Munich also became a symbol **25** of the ignominious appeasement of Britain and France. In Munich's Führerbau, a meeting took place between Prime ministers Neville Chamberlain and Edouard Daladier, during which they negotiated the dismemberment of Czechoslovakia with Hitler and Mussolini. Later, Chamberlain obtained a signed piece of paper from the Führer, that the British leader waved at his people as a guarantee of 'peace in our time'.

War and Peace

One spark of resistance from wartime Munich came when two students, Hans and Sophie Scholl, courageously distributed anti-Hitler 'White Rose' leaflets. But brother and sister were betrayed and executed.

World War II brought 71 air raids to the city, killing 6,000 and wounding 16,000. Bombardments were most intense in 1944, heavily damaging the Frauenkirche, St Peter's and St Michael's churches and large parts of the Residenz and Alte Pinakothek. The Brown House was destroyed but, ironically, the majority of Hitler's other buildings were left intact.

The post-war reconstruction was a triumph of hard work together with fiercely loyal attachment to the great traditions of Munich's past. Monuments, palaces and churches were all restored with meticulous care. Traditionally open to the arts and to good living in general, Munich expanded and became Germany's third-largest city (total population 1,207,000), welcoming many Berliners and refugees from the former eastern territories.

The 1972 Olympic Games launched Munich on the world stage as the 'Metropolis with a Heart', and an outstanding network of sports facilities was established for the event. The city has continued to build on its international reputation as a city of culture with a year-round programme of performing-arts productions, including concerts and open-air opera in the beautiful surroundings of the great palaces and monuments. Visitors to Munich can be sure of a taste of good living – Bavarian-style.

What to See

Munich has two enormous assets as far as the visitor is concerned. First, a large majority of the city's museums, monuments, palaces and churches are concentrated in the Innenstadt (inner city), which makes Munich a great town for walking. Second, the superb public transport system, which incorporates buses, trams, underground (*U-Bahn*) and surface trains (*S-Bahn*), brings all the other sights within easy reach.

Rather than dealing with the complicated business of driving your car round town, find yourself a parking place on the outskirts of town -- parking is almost impossible in the centre – and save the car for excursions. If you walk wherever you can, you'll see more of the town's bustling street life and drop in more easily on the outdoor cafés. You'll be able to indulge in the pleasure of discovering Munich's unexpected courtyard vistas and its hidden alleyways. You'll also happen upon numerous little bars and shops tucked away in odd corners that you would completely miss in a car.

So, apart from the section devoted to excursions, Munich is presented here in the form of a series of walks.

The Altes Rathaus on Marienplatz, a reconstruction of the original 15th-century town hall.

Innenstadt

Munich long ago expanded beyond the confines of its medieval boundaries, and the old city wall has now disappeared. However, the remains of three gates survive to indicate the perimeter of the inner city – Isartor, Karlstor and Sendlinger Tor – as well as Odeonsplatz, a rendezvous for salt traders setting off in the 14th century for northern Germany. Ever since Munich's earliest beginnings, Marienplatz has been at the heart of it all.

MARIENPLATZ TO THEATINERSTRASSE

Until the middle of the 19th century, **Marienplatz** was the place where the wheat market was held. The square was the obvious site for the town hall and was the place where criminals were hanged. Marienplatz was also the focus for the most extravagant wedding Munich has ever seen – that of Duke Wilhelm V to Renata of Lorraine in 1568. It was the inevitable choice for the central

junction of the U-Bahn and S-Bahn system in 1972.

Graced with its tubs of flowers and outdoor cafés, Marienplatz today forms part of an attractive pedestrian zone. It is the home of the **Mariensäule** (Column of the Virgin Mary), erected in 1638 by Maximilian I in gratitude for the town's deliverance from the Plague after its defeat by the Swedes during the Thirty Years' War. At the base of the column are a basilisk, dragon, serpent and lion – which represent plague, hunger, heresy and war – each being vanquished by heroic child-angels. On the top of the monument is the majestic figure of Mary, who watches over Munich. Holding Jesus in her left arm and a sceptre in her right, she is a reminder of Munich's religious foundation.

The square also contains the partially reconstructed 19th-century Fischbrunnen monument. Young butchers used to leap into the bronze fountain at the end of their apprenticeship, but today the tradition is kept up only by Fasching (carnival) revellers or happy soccer fans.

MUNICH HIGHLIGHTS

(See also Museum and Art Gallery Highlights on p.55)

Asamkirche, Sendlinger Strasse 62. The idiosyncratic Church of St Johann Nepomuk, with flamboyant rococo façade and interior. *U-bahn 1, 3, 62 Sendlinger Tor.* (See p.42)

Bavaria Film Studios, Bavariafilmplatz 7, Geiselgasteig, tel. 649 37 67. Guided tours of the German film studios take place daily from 1 March to 31 October. Stunt shows are staged on Saturday, Sunday and Friday at 11.30am, 1pm and 2.30pm. *U-bahn 1, 2 to Silberhornstraße, then Tram 25.*

Englischer Garten: beautiful winding park along the River Isar. Don't miss the city's largest beer garden next to the Chinese Tower. *U-bahn Giselastraße or Münchener Freiheit.* (See p.50)

Frauenkirche: one of Munich's most identifiable landmarks, the Cathedral dominates the skyline with its twin domes. (See p.31)

Hofbräuhaus, Platzl, tel. 221 676. This famous and atmospheric beer hall should not be missed. Go for dinner or for some after-dinner entertainment. (See p.37)

Marienplatz: the heart of Munich and one of the finest town squares in Europe. 11am for the 43-bell Glockenspiel of the Neues Rathaus. (see p.28)

Nyphenburg Palace, tel. 179 08/0. A beautiful building with wonderful gardens, and associated museums. Open daily except Monday, 10am to 12.30pm and 1.30 to 4pm, to 5pm April to October. *Tram 12, bus 21.* (See p.84)

Residenz, Max-Joseph Platz, tel. 290 671. Formerly the residence of the Wittelsbachs, it is now an incredible museum with 112 rooms and 10 Treasuries. Open daily except Monday, 10am to 4.30pm. *U-bahn 3, 4, 5, 6 Odeonsplatz, tram 19, bus 53.* (See p.59)

St Peters: the city's oldest church, dating before 1158. Make the long climb to the top for a breathtaking view of the city. (See p.35)

Viktualienmarkt: just south of the Marienplatz, this colourful market is the place to go for anything food-related. One of the most colourful areas of Munich. (See p.43)

Standing at the eastern end of Marienplatz is the almost too picturesque **Altes Rathaus** (Old Town Hall), a gay example of Munich's efforts to reconstruct, rather than replace, the remnants of its venerable history. The dove-grey façade, amber-tiled steeple and graceful little spires of this Gothic-style edifice capture the spirit of the 15th-century original designed by Jörg von Halsbach (also called Jörg Ganghofer), though it isn't an exact replica. In any case, with the addition over the centuries of a Baroque onion-shaped cupola and then a too-conscientious 'regothification', the building that was destroyed by Allied bombs was probably further from the original than what you see today. Apart from a banqueting hall on an upper floor, the Altes Rathaus fulfills a mainly decorative function.

The daily business of city government takes place at the **Neues Rathaus** (New Town Hall) on the northern side of Marienplatz. This is a classic example of 19th-century neo-Gothic architecture – proud and self-assertive, its façade elaborately decorated with the statues of kings, princes and dukes, saints, allegorical figures and characters from the folklore of Munich. The tower is around 80m (260ft) high. Its main attraction, apart from the splendid view – if you want to take the lift to the top – is the 43-bell Glockenspiel (carillon) which puts on a show daily at 11am. Two groups of figures appear, one group re-enacting the tournament held during the wedding of Duke Wilhelm V and Renata of Lorraine and the other, underneath, re-creating the cooper's dance (*Schäfflertanz*) which was performed to exorcize the plague of 1517. In the evening, at 9pm, a night-watchman with lantern blows his horn and an angel of peace blesses the little Munich monk (Münchner Kindl).

Now go along Weinstrasse (around the corner at the west end of the Neues Rathaus) and left along Sporerstrasse to the **Frauenkirche** – its full title is Domkirche zu Unserer Lieben Frau (Cathedral Church of Our Lady). This building, perhaps more than any other, symbolizes Munich, its gold-tipped, bulbous domes on twin brick towers dominating the skyline. The church, is an austere, unadorned Gothic structure, and was built between 1468 and

Munich's efficient network of trams and underground trains makes child's-play of sightseeing.

1488 by Jörg von Halsbach. The Italian Renaissance domes are an addition of 1524. After extensive reconstruction work on the exterior, the church is now once again open daily.

The stark interior was reconstructed from the rubble of World War II bombardments – a truly heroic work of restoration. The original Gothic windows in the choir, stored in safety during the war, give an impression of the church's former glory. Fine sculptures of the Apostles and Prophets also escaped destruction and adorn the choir as before. They were created by Erasmus Grasser in 1502. An admirable altarpiece of 1483 by Friedrich Pacher, the *Baptism of Christ*, hangs in the north chapel. It is flanked by Jan Polack's panels which depict Jesus on the Mount of Olives and his arrest, crucifixion and burial. Notice, too, the 17th-century funerary monument of Emperor Ludwig the Bavarian, who died in 1347.

Just outside the church, the granite fountain in Frauenplatz strikes a modern note. A waterfall plays, and stones are set out in the shape of an amphitheatre to provide seating.

Augustinerstrasse, west of the square, leads to Neuhauser Strasse and to what was once the church of the Augustinians. The building became a customs house in the time of Napoleon and then, in 1966, a

The distincitve twin domes of the Frauenkirche dominate the Munich skyline.

hunting and fishing museum, the Deutsches Jagd- und Fis- chereimuseum. Proclaimed by a wild boar in bronze, the col- lection will fascinate hunters, anglers and children alike.

Go further along pedestrian- zoned Neuhauser Strasse to the 16th-century **St Michael's**, an Italian Renaissance church with Baroque overtones – the first of its kind in Germany – largely designed by the Dutch architect Friedrich Sustris. St Michael epitomizes the com- bative spirit of the Counter- Reformation, and it is fitting that the Wittelsbach dukes and German emperors – the secu- lar defenders of the faith – are depicted on the gabled façade. Above the entrance, third fig- ure from the right, stands the church's patron, Duke Wil- helm V (with a scale model of St Michael's Church in his hand). Il Gesù, in Rome, was the inspiration for the Baroque interior of St Michael's, which surpasses the former in its masterful lighting.

Karlstor, a city gate dating from the 14th century, links Neuhauser Strasse to the busy Karlsplatz, which is popularly known as the Stachus after an innkeeper named Eustachius Föderl. The **Stachus** conceals a veritable city of underground shops, which extends from the exit of the U- and S-Bahn sta- tion. Walk north to Lenbach- platz and you'll find the city's loveliest fountain, the **Wittels- bacher Brunnen**, which was built in neo-Baroque style by Adolf von Hildebrand at the end of the 19th century.

Pacellistrasse, to the east of Lenbachplatz, takes you past the Baroque façade of the **Dreifaltigkeitskirche** (Trinity Church). In 1704 a young girl, Anna Maria Lindmayr, dreamt that Munich would be invaded and destroyed unless a new church were constructed. Sure enough, the next year, during the War of the Spanish Succes- sion, Austrian soldiers arrived. Although work on the Drei- faltigkeitskirche did not begin until 1711, the town was saved from destruction.

Promenadeplatz is noted for the elegance of Palais Montge- las. This neo-Classical build- ing today forms part of the **33** classy Bayerischer Hof hotel, where you might like to refresh yourself with an expensive drink at the bar.

Continue north along Kardinal-Faulhaber-Strasse past the Palais Porcia, one of Munich's first Baroque palaces, now a bank, to the **Erzbischöfliches** Palais (Archbishop's Palace) at number 7, a triumph of Rococo harmony with especially fine stucco work. Originally known as Palais Holnstein, it's the only 18th-century palace built by François Cuvilliés (see p.41) to have survived intact to the present day.

Why not end your walk in the shopping arcades of Theatinerstrasse and spoil yourself in a *Konditorei*, a café specializing in pastries and coffee.

ISARTORPLATZ TO PLATZL

The sturdy Isartor, in its restored form, is the only city gate which retains its original 14th-century dimensions. Put up in the days when the Bavarian Duke Ludwig IV was Holy Roman Emperor, a later fresco

of 1835 on the gate shows the emperor returning triumphantly from victory over the Habsburgs. The Isartor now serves as a rather overgrown traffic island, but one of the towers houses a roof-top café and the Valentin-Museum, devoted to the famous cabaret comic of 1920s Munich, Karl Valentin (see box, p.48).

From Isartor, go along Tal, a shopping street that takes you to **Heiliggeistkirche** (Church of the Holy Spirit). This 14th-century Gothic structure was extensively altered to suit the Baroque tastes of the 1720s. The two styles come together perfectly in the **Marienaltar** – a lovely wooden sculpture of 1450, the *Hammerthaler Muttergottes* (Hammerthal Mother of God) originally from the Lake Tegernsee monastery, set in an opulent gilded Baroque framework. The reconstructed high altar preserves a fine pair of *Adoring Angels* from 1730 by Johann Georg Greiff.

View of St Peter's church, with its distinctive tower, from across the Viktalienmarkt.

West of Heiliggeistkirche, with an entrance on Rindermarkt, is **St Peter's**, the oldest church in Munich, dating from before the foundation of the city itself in 1158. The original structure gave way to a building in the Romanesque style, **35** fathers of the Church. It was restored from the remnants of the 18th-century original, inspired by Bernini's altar for St Peter's in Rome. Egid Quirin Asam (see p.41) was the designer of the ensemble, incorporating Erasmus Grasser's *St Peter*. The gilded wood figures of the Church fathers are the masterly work of Egid Quirin.

Leading up to the altar are splendid Rococo choir stalls. You'll also see five of Jan Polack's Late Gothic paintings which once adorned the altar. The paintings show Peter healing the lame, enthroned, at sea, in prison and on the cross. Also from the Late Gothic period is the Schrenk-Altar, a fine early 15th-century sandstone relief of the Crucifixion and the Day of Judgment.

Coming out, duck along little Burgstrasse past the Altes Rathaus. Stop at number 5 to

succeeded in time by a Gothic church which boasted a twin-steepled tower. Everything but the tower was destroyed in the great fire of 1327 and a new Gothic structure went up. This was remodelled along Renaissance lines in the 17th century, and a new tower with a single steeple was created. Destroyed in the war, St Peter's has been faithfully reconstructed, down to the asymmetrically placed clocks on the tower. (Follow the crowd to the top for a stunning view of the inner city.)

The crowning piece of the light, bright interior is the **high altar** glorifying Peter and the admire the **Weinstadl**, one of only a few Gothic houses still left in Munich, once the home of the town clerk and now a tavern. Built in about 1550, it has a neatly restored, leafy courtyard and staircase tower.

The **Alter Hof** is a miracle of inner-city tranquillity. The peaceful, tree-shaded square presents an exquisite panorama of medieval buildings. The reconstructed Burgtor (City Gate) nearby, and quaint little Affenturm (Monkey Tower) – incorporated in the west wing – recapture the atmosphere of the Wittelsbachs' first Munich residence as it was in the 15th century. The splendid heraldic painting on the tower came to light in the 1960s.

The Hof was originally built around 1255 on what was then the north-east corner of town, in defence against foreign invaders, as well as the city's own unruly burghers. It was superseded by the more massive Residenz. The buildings suffered more at the hands of 19th-century urban developers than during the 20th-century bombing, but the careful re-construction of the surviving south and west wings gives an idea of their former grandeur.

Turn right on Pfisterstrasse to Platzl (Little Square), the site of a building of no great architectural distinction but, nevertheless, the most publi-cized monument in Munich, the **Hofbräuhaus** beer hall.

Duke Wilhelm V founded a brewery in the Alter Hof in 1589 to avoid paying the high prices for imported beer from Hanover – beer having always been just as much an aristo-cratic as a plebeian drink in Bavaria. It replaced wine as the staple alcoholic beverage after the Bavarian vineyards were destroyed by the cruel winters of the 13th and 14th centuries, making way for the sturdier hop and barley crops.

The brewery was first estab-lished in the royal bath house, and moved to more spacious quarters on Platzl in 1644. The Hofbräuhaus itself was built in 1896, after the brewery was transferred to the other side of the River Isar. It soon became the most prestigious of Mu-nich's many political beer-hall **37** arenas. In fact, in November 1921 Hitler's storm troops first gained notoriety in what became known as the '*Schlacht im Hofbräuhaus*' (Battle of the Hofbräuhaus). Today, the huge beer hall, with its long tables and oom-pah-pah music, is a magnet for tourists. Don't be surprised to see dogs sitting with their owners in the Hofbrauhaus or in any other city restaurants – it's perfectly acceptable here in Munich!

ODEONSPLATZ TO MAXIMILANSTRASSE

Odeonsplatz joins the inner city to Schwabing and the university. At this spot Ludwig I opened up the overcrowded heart of town to the more airy *Vorstadt* – Schwabing then being no more than a suburb.

This particularly airy and 'liberating' walk begins in the Italian Renaissance-style Hofgarten (Court Garden), now restored and replanted with the chestnut trees, flower beds and fountains specified in the original 17th-century plan. In the centre stands a 12-sided temple dedicated to Diana, topped by a bronze statue of Bavaria. The arcades that line the garden house art galleries and cafés, and are decorated with frescoes of historic scenes that feature the Wittelsbachs. To the north (Galeriestrasse 4) is a fascinating **Theatermuseum**, worth visiting for the display of famous set designs from Munich's rich theatrical past.

Now turn and look southwest across the Hofgarten to capture the delightful vista that helps to give Munich its peculiarly Mediterranean flavour – the twin towers and dome of the splendid **Theatinerkirche**. This Italian Baroque church was built between 1663 and 1688 by two Italian architects, Agostino Barelli and Enrico Zuccalli. The façade was completed later by Cuvilliés.

Perhaps because it was built to celebrate the birth of a baby boy to Princess Henriette Adelaide, a feeling of jubilation animates the church's rich decoration – with sprigs of ornamental vines, acanthus leaves and rosettes in the most spirited Italian Baroque style, and its wonderful grey-and-white stucco embellishments in the cupola. Notice, as well, the triumphant pulpit, the high altar (a copy of one destroyed by bombs) and, to the left, the Kajetan altar. This last was dedicated to St Kajetan, founder of the Theatine Order commemorated in the church's title.

Just across the street, facing Odeonsplatz, is the **Feldherrnhalle** (Hall of the Generals), a 19th-century monument to a number of Bavarian military leaders, including the Belgian-born Count Johann Tilly – a hero in the Thirty Years' War, and Prince Karl-Philipp von Wrede, who achieved victory over the French in 1814. Less gloriously, it was the rendez-vous for Nazi storm troops in Hitler's unsuccessful putsch of 1923 and was subsequently a focus for marches commemorating the event. Reinforcing the Italian atmosphere of the area, though with less of a light touch, the building is modelled after the Late Gothic Loggia dei Lanzi in Florence.

Nearby, in Residenzstrasse, is found **Preysing-Palais**, the most lavishly ornamented private Rococo palace in Munich. Begun in 1723 by Joseph Effner, the Residenzstrasse façade was the only part to survive World War II, but the restoration of other parts was masterful. Take a look inside at the imposing ceremonial staircase.

At the other end of the street lies another jewel of 18th-century architecture, the **Hauptpostamt** or Main Post Office,

Temple of Diana in the formal Hofgarten, planted according to the original 17th-century plans.

and formerly the Palais Törring-Jettenbach. The northern façade was given a face-lift in the 19th century to fit in with the classical demands of the Residenz and Nationaltheater on Maximilianstrasse. But the original Baroque doorway can be seen inside.

Completely rebuilt in 1963, the **Nationaltheater** is a faithful copy of the original building of 1818 – a Greek-temple design by Karl von Fischer.

The spacious **Max-Joseph-Platz** is named after the king whose statue sits in the centre. The fourth Max-Joseph of the Wittelsbach dynasty and the first – thanks to Napoleon – to be king, wanted what he considered to be a more dignified standing pose. Unfortunately, he died before the statue was completed and his son Ludwig I accepted the seated version.

The statue was put alongside the greatest monument of Max-Joseph's family, the Wittelsbach **Residenz**. In 1385 the citizenry revolted, driving the dukes to construct safer lodgings than the Alter Hof (see p.37). More than five centuries later, in 1918, another group of rebellious citizens pounded on the Residenz doors during the revolution that resulted in the short-lived Bavarian republic. The Wittelsbachs had to move out once again, and this time it was for good.

Musician on Odeonsplatz brings Munich's rich musical culture out onto the streets.

Many of the Bavarian dukes and kings were passionate art collectors and keen builders. The Residenz, now a museum, shows just how powerful and immensely wealthy the proud Bavarian principality grew to be. To view the exterior, enter via Residenzstrasse and walk through the seven courtyards to the Cuvilliéstheater – within the Residenz but not included on museum tours.

The splendid **Cuvilliéstheater**, or Altes Residenztheater, is one of the most enchanting playhouses in the world. Like its architect François de Cuvilliés, a dwarf from the Spanish Netherlands, the theatre is tiny, seating only 450. But its festive intimacy turns every performance into a cosy gala. The four-tiered, horseshoe-shaped auditorium basks in gilded Rococo décor with hosts of Greek nymphs, gods and goddesses and, with marvellous incongruity, an American Indian girl with her bow and arrows. The acoustics are warm and golden – totally suited to the Mozart works that have been played here for the past 200 years.

The Cuvilliéstheater owes its existence to planning and foresight. In 1943, its stucco ornamentation and sculptures were dismantled. Some 30,000 pieces were carried away and stored in the vaults of various castles around Munich. Only six weeks later the theatre was gutted by fire bombs. However, fifteen years elapsed before all the pieces were brought out of hiding and reassembled.

SENDLINGER TOR TO VIKTUALIENMARKT

The walk from Sendlinger Tor takes you through the busy shopping area of Sendlinger Strasse, and past the municipal museum to the open-air market next to St Peter's church. Only two hexagonal towers remain from the 14th-century **Sendlinger Tor** (City Gate).

Facing north-east, follow the left fork along Sendlinger Strasse to **Asamhaus** (number 61) where Egid Quirin Asam, a master sculptor and architect of the 18th century, lived. He was assisted in the decoration of the building by his brother, **41**

Cosmas Damian, who specialized in fresco painting. The ornate forenames of the brothers are suited to the rich Baroque style favoured by the two.

Stand on the opposite side of Sendlinger Strasse and look at the marvellously intricate façade of the house, built in 1733. Secure in their Catholic faith, the Asam brothers happily mixed pagan and Christian figures in their decorative schemes. Just below the roof to the right (directly above the doorway) you'll see a representation in stucco of heaven and the monogram of Christ. Below that appears the seated figure of Mary. To the left is a vine-bedecked Olympus, and Apollo is accompanied by the triumphant gods of Fame and Fortune. Pegasus, the flying horse, leaps up to them, while, lower down, a riot of nymphs and satyrs dance around the Muses of painting, sculpture and architecture. The original doorway, on which are depicted scenes from the Old and New Testaments, is now displayed in the Bavarian National Museum (see p.63).

Enormous diligence and ingenuity marks the decoration of Asamhaus. It also confirms the brothers' lighthearted devotion to the good life and the inspiration of their religion.

The ultimate demonstration of this can be seen next door in the Asams' private church of St Johann Nepomuk, which was originally linked to Egid Quirin's house. This church is popularly known as **Asamkirche**, and was completed in 1746. Built at Egid Quirin's own expense, its design was free from the constraints of a patron's demands. The result is a subjective celebration of faith and life.

Its variegated marble façade serves as a street-altar for the passers-by on busy Sendlinger Strasse. The church incorporates unhewn rocks originally intended for a fountain, and a statue of John of Nepomuk, a Bohemian saint popular in the 18th century, stands over the porch. Inside, the **high altar** leads the eye up to a large Crucifixion dominated by a representation of God the Father, wearing the papal crown.

The impressive four-storey **Altes Hackerhaus** is on the corner of Hackenstrasse. This rare surviving example of a private dwelling in the classical style has a succession of nine Doric, Ionic and Corinthian pillars running along each façade, and beautiful, historic living rooms. Go further along Hackenstrasse to the corner of Hotterstrasse, where Munich's oldest operating tavern, called Gaststätte zur Hundskugel, has been serving beer since 1440.

If you double back across Sendlinger Strasse, you'll find St-Jakobs-Platz and the **Münchner Stadtmuseum** (Municipal Museum; see p.64). To the east of this fascinating museum lies one of the most colourful locations in Munich and a magnet for all who love food – the **Viktualienmarkt**. The city's central food market has been doing business here since 1807. Stroll around the enticing stalls with their myriad cheeses and exotic spices, breads and meats. The cornucopia of vegetables and fruit prove better than anything else that Munich is a crossroads of northern and southern Europe, and a gateway to the East, too.

The cheerful atmosphere of the market makes it the perfect place for annual performances of the Marketwomen's Dance, held on Shrove Tuesday. It's also the scene of a number of lively celebrations around the flower-bedecked maypole.

A colourful cornucopia of flowers, fruit and vegetables on the Viktualienmarkt.

Around Königsplatz

To the north-west of the inner city, beyond the Alter Botanischer Garten, **Königsplatz** represents a convergence of the noblest and basest aspirations arising from the past several hundred years of Munich's history. When Ludwig I was still crown prince, he visualized the square as a second Acropolis, a vast open space surrounded by classical temples. There was no particular reason for the choice of this site, no junction of roads, for example. Ludwig simply overrode the customary demands of urban planning, and soon had men working on widening the stately Brienner Strasse, the street which took the royal family from the Residenz to Nymphenburg Palace.

With Leo von Klenze working as his architect, Ludwig turned the square into a grass-covered, tree-lined haven of tranquillity. A hundred years later, Hitler cut down the trees and paved over the grass for the troops and armoured cars of his military parades. (The pompous Nazi **Ehrentempel**, or Temple of Honour, which stood at the eastern end of the square, was deliberately blown up by the Allied military engineers in 1945.) Today, at last, Königsplatz is returning to its original serenity, and the pastoral greenery is back.

The U-Bahn station brings you out beside the **Propyläen** (Propylaeum), modelled after the entranceway to the Acropolis in Athens. Unlike the original entranceway, this splendid monument to Ludwig's sublime imperviousness to functional considerations does not lead anywhere, for it closes off Königsplatz rather than providing access to the square. Despite the Doric columns, it's not even authentically Greek, since the central 'gateway' is flanked by two Egyptian-style pylons or towers. The friezes that decorate them on the other hand show the Wittelsbachs' special attachment to all things Greek. They show representations of the Greek war of liberation from the Turks and the Greek people paying homage to Ludwig's son Otto when he was made their king in 1832.

Before visiting the monuments on Königsplatz, carry on walking past the Propyläen up to **Lenbachhaus** on Luisenstrasse. This elegant ochre-coloured villa, constructed in the 1880s, is based on the style of Renaissance Florence, and was rebuilt after World War II. Franz von Lenbach, a wealthy academic painter, and highly regarded amongst the German aristocracy, built himself this showy palace with the fortune he accumulated from his art. Today the villa houses the excellent **Städtische Galerie** of

*B*uilt in Italian Renaissance style, Lenbachhaus brings a mediterranean air to Munich.

19th- and 20th-century art (see p.83). Coffee is served on the terrace or in the pleasant garden, and there is a little park just opposite in which you can play open-air chess on giant stone boards.

Situated on the south side of Königsplatz is the **Staatliche Antikensammlungen** (Classical Art Collections, see p.81), which seems rather clumsily **45** designed, with its Corinthian columns set on an excessively elevated pedestal. Just across the square stands the companion building, the **Glyptothek** (Sculpture Museum, see p.81). It was designed in 1815 by von Klenze to display Ludwig I's large collection of Greek and Roman sculpture, and was the

The Glyptothek was built to house Ludwig I's extensive collections of classical sculpture.

first building to be planned for use as a public museum.

If you cross over Gabelsberger Strasse, you come to another venerable art institution, the **Alte Pinakothek**. Ludwig commissioned von Klenze to provide a design for a monumental museum in the style of an Italian Renaissance palace. Reconstruction in 1958 preserved the spacious layout of galleries and cabinets and introduced some excellent lighting. Now the gallery is again in need of renovation, and will be closed until 1997 (see p.54, Neue Pinakothek).

North of nearby Theresienstrasse is situated the strikingly modern **Neue Pinakothek** building, opened to the public in 1981. The work of Alexander von Branca, the elegant grey sandstone and granite structure replaces the original building destroyed in World War II. Extensive skylights provide superb natural lighting. The style of the architecture is a break with the Alte Pinakothek's classical traditions, but it achieves a total harmony nonetheless. (For a description of Munich's museums, see pp.54-83.)

In case you think it is facile to relentlessly attack Hitler's legacy in Munich, take a look for yourself at two surviving examples of his architectural contribution to the city: sited at the east end of Königsplatz, they are known as Führer's Buildings (*Führerbauten*). At Arcisstrasse 12, now a music academy (*Musikhochschule*), Hitler received Chamberlain and Daladier, the British and French prime ministers, who accepted the infamous Munich agreement of 1938 (see p.26). Meiserstrasse 10 today houses important archaeological and art-historical institutions, but it was built in 1933 as an administrative centre for the Nazi Party. These grim, bunker-like blocks, designed by Paul Ludwig Troost under the obsessive supervision of Hitler himself, ironically survived the American bombardments which severely damaged the historic Glyptothek and Staatliche Antikensammlungen.

Rather than finish the walk on this sombre note, continue down Meiserstrasse to the **Alter Botanischer Garten**. Although the town's major botanical garden has now been transferred to Nymphenburg Palace (see p.88), the lawns here still make for a pleasant stroll. Take a seat by the Neptune Fountain and look over the trees for a view of the two cupolas of the Frauenkirche. It's amazing to think that the people of Munich found time to lay out this lovely tranquil spot right in the middle of the Napoleonic Wars.

Schwabing

The Schwabing district is one of a select group of places – including Chelsea in London, Montparnasse in Paris and Greenwich Village in New York – which have been described as 'not so much a place as a state of mind'.

Begin your walk symbolically – Munich loves symbols – at the **Siegestor** (Victory Gate), which marks the southern boundary of Schwabing. This triumphal arch was designed for Ludwig I as a monument to the Bavarian army. In 1944 the arch was badly damaged, and in 1958 only partially restored, leaving the scars of war and a new inscription on the south side: *Dem Sieg geweiht, im Krieg zerstört, zum Frieden mahnend* (Dedicated to victory, destroyed in war, exhorting to peace). More than any other part of Munich, Schwabing epitomizes a break with military traditions.

Walk to the entrance of the University and visit the little square named Geschwister-Scholl-Platz, in memory of the brother and sister who died in the struggle against Hitler (see p.26). Across the street is St Ludwig's, a neo-Romanesque church noted for the gigantic fresco of the *Last Judgement*

Valentin's Day

Although little known outside Germany, Karl Valentin was regarded by connoisseurs like the dramatist Bertolt Brecht as a comic genius equal to Charlie Chaplin. While resident in Munich in the early twenties, Brecht went almost every night to watch Valentin's portrayal of the clownish, working-class characters of peasant origin who were so peculiar to the city.

Valentin quickly attracted the attention of Schwabing's artists and intellectuals, who loved his insane, surreal logic. One of his most celebrated sketches portrayed an attempt to house birds in an aquarium and fish in a bird-cage.

in the choir, by Peter Cornelius (1836). After Michelangelo's in the Sistine Chapel, it's the world's second-largest fresco at 18m (60ft) by 11m (37ft).

At night the bohemian spirit of Schwabing animates wide and breezy **Leopoldstrasse**, beginning north of Siegestor. The great writers and artists that frequented the street in the past may have disappeared, but the art galleries and cafés are still going strong, and there is an underlying sense of excitement as you stroll along what is jokingly referred to as Boulevard Leopold. Having provided a focus for the avant-garde of Jugendstil and the Blaue Reiter, Schwabing now serves as the meeting place for the talents of the new German cinema. You may well catch a glimpse of the latest directors or actors in favour, or at least those aspiring to stardom.

On finding Münchener Freiheit, road junction and U-Bahn stop, follow Feilitzschstrasse to **Wedekindplatz**, a centre of theatre, cabaret and café life reminiscent of the golden past. Continue on to Werneckstrasse

*E*thnic jewellery for sale in Schwabing, the bohemian district of Munich.

and to **Suresnes-Schlösschen** (Little Château), which is now the Catholic Academy. It was built in 1718 for Prince Elector Max Emanuel as a reminder of the ten happy years he spent at the French château of the same name during the War of the Spanish Succession. Remodelled several times in the 19th century, some of the stucco work of the original Baroque structure can still be seen. **49**

Englischer Garten Area

From Schwabing, head east to the lovely **Englischer Garten**. Opened in 1793, the park was the brainchild of an American-born adventurer who had sided with the British in the American Revolution. Better known to the Bavarians as Count Rumford (see p.17), Benjamin Thompson drew his inspiration from the famous English landscape gardeners Capability Brown and William Chambers. In fact, the Chinesischer Turm (Chinese Tower), a decorative pagoda that functions as a bandstand in the popular beer garden, owes a great deal to Chambers' Cantonese Pagoda in London's Kew Gardens.

Rumford and his German associate Ludwig von Sckell broke with the French tradition – which was favoured by the Bavarian aristocracy – of gardens with geometric avenues, and carefully sculptured trees and hedges, preferring a 'natural' grouping of hills, dells and babbling brooks. In keeping with the spirit of their revolutionary populist ideas, they decided to create a garden for Munich's poorer inhabitants. Prince Karl Theodor had been under the impression that the Englischer Garten would be an elaborate extension of the Hofgarten, until he saw pigs and cattle grazing where his lords had once hunted for pheasant and stags, and potato patches in place of exotic flowers.

Today the pigs and potatoes are long gone, but the natural landscaping is still a joy for picnickers, lovers and all other visitors. The Monopteros (love temple) atop a grassy mound south of the Chinese Tower is an attractive focal point from which to admire the splendid view of the old city.

The gardens stretch almost 5km (3 miles) to the north, and make a lovely walk alongside the swiftly flowing River Isar. Stroll up to the Kleinhesseloher See, a boating pond, or to the little Eisbach, a branch of the Isar rushing helter-skelter under Tivoli Bridge as fast as a mountain rapid. The river encourages a particularly breakneck version of wind-surfing –

a great spectator sport. However, if the mere sight of such activity exhausts you, head for the pretty Japanese Tea House (in the south-west corner), donated by Japan to commemorate the 1972 Olympic Games.

Just beyond the Tea House, on the southern edge of the garden at Prinzregentenstrasse 1, stands the **Haus der Kunst** (House of Art), a venue for temporary exhibitions and the location of the Staatsgalerie moderner Kunst (State Modern Art Gallery; see p.83).

The Haus der Kunst is another building of the Hitler era that the Allied bombardments missed. Originally known as the Haus der deutschen Kunst (House of German Art), it was a temple to Hitler's personal vision of a truly German art. The monotonous construction, again by Paul Ludwig Troost,

There are plenty of opportunities for walking or cycling along the lovely river Isar.

Take a break at the Chinesischer Turm, one of the city's most popular beer gardens.

was soon endowed with some popular nicknames, which included 'Münchner Kunstterminus' (Munich Art Terminal) and 'Palazzo Kitschi'.

Another museum is to be found further along Prinzregentenstrasse, the **Bayerisches Nationalmuseum** (the Bavar-**52**

ian National Museum; see p.63). From here, walk across Prinzregentenbrücke, crossing the River Isar, to the winged **Friedensengel** (Peace Angel). High on her pillar, she surveys Prinzregententerrasse, a lovely promenade in Florentine style surrounded by gardens. Begun in 1896, the monument celebrates the 25 years of peace that followed from the German defeat of the French in 1871. Portraits of the architects of that peace – Bismarck, Kaisers Wilhelm I and II, and the generals Moltke and von der Tann – decorate the monument. The mosaics of *Peace, War, Victory* and the *Blessings of Culture* indicate the rather ambiguous nature of the celebration.

There's nothing ambiguous, however, about the charming **Villa Stuck**, at Prinzregentenstrasse 60, which was built in 1898 for the last in Munich's line of painter-princes, Franz von Stuck. He amassed a fortune rivalling that of Lenbach by astutely combining the new artistic trends of Jugendstil symbolism with the prevailing salon taste, which demanded a certain luxury spiced with just a dash of decadence. His opulent villa is the perfect setting for the Jugendstil Museum, which is now housed there. All the interior decoration and furniture date from the turn of the century. The house is guarded by Stuck's imposing equestrian *Amazone*, and is often used as a venue for temporary exhibitions, usually of modern or contemporary art.

To the south lies the phenomenal **Deutsches Museum** (see p.61) of science and technology. On the west bank of the Isar, opposite the museum, rises the controversial European Patent Office *(Europäisches Patentamt)*. While this black steel-and-glass structure has found many admirers, others have protested against the demolition of the old neighbourhood that stood in its way.

Free for All

During Schwabing's heyday at the turn of the 20th century, artists and writers flocked to this bohemian area of Munich. Thomas Mann lived here, as did Frank Wedekind and Bertolt Brecht, Wassily Kandinsky and Paul Klee, as well as Franz Marc, Rainer Maria Rilke and symbolist poet Stefan George.

A countess-turned-bohemian, Franziska zu Reventlow, chronicled the area's free love, free art and freedom for all in her novels, dying penniless of the suitably romantic illness of tuberculosis. Schwabing was also home to the biting satirical weekly *Simplicissimus* and to the art magazine *Jugend*, which gave its name to the German version of Art Nouveau – Jugendstil.

In 1919, the 'Coffeehouse Anarchists', dramatist Ernst Toller and poet Erich Mühsam, took power after the assassination of the prime minister, Kurt Eisner. For all of six days – until the communists pushed the poets out – Schwabing ruled Bavaria, proclaiming the republic a 'meadow full of flowers'.

Museums

The number and diversity of museums and galleries in Munich attest to the city's importance as a cultural centre. See the brief listing opposite for an overview of the highlights.

 NEUE PINAKOTHEK

Barer Strasse 27, U-bahn 2, Königsplatz; Straßenbahn 27. Following the temporary closure of the Alte Pinakothek for renovation, this gallery has been completely reorganised to incorporate the most important masterpieces of the Alte Pinakothek collections. These include old German Masters, outstanding examples of the Flemish, Dutch, Italian, Spanish and French Schools, and 19th-century paintings. The Alte Pinakothek is due to reopen in 1997.

An unusual feature of the gallery is that the layout has been organised from a chronological standpoint rather than by country and artistic movement. This enables the visitor to compare the interpretations of the different contemporary schools through the centuries.

One of the most outstanding German pieces is the *Kirchenväteraltar* (Altarpiece of the Church Fathers), painted in about 1483 by Michael Pacher. This marvellous polyptych of the saints Jerome, Augustine, Gregory and Ambrose was acquired from the South Tyrol during the French Revolution.

Geburt Christi (the Birth of Christ) is by Stephan Lochner of the 15th-century Cologne School.

Pieter Brueghel the Elder produced *Das Schlaraffenland* (Fool's Paradise) in 1567. The artist depicts a soldier, a peasant and a scholar sprawled on the ground – a bitter depiction of ignorance and sloth, which Brueghel considered to be the evils of Spanish occupation.

Works by Roger van der Weyden are displayed alongside those of his Italian contemporary Filippo Lippi, from the mid-15th century. Hans Memling's *Freuden Mariae* (Joys of Mary), and Martin Schongauer's *Heilige Familie* (The Holy Family) contrast

MUSEUM AND ART GALLERY HIGHLIGHTS

(See also Munich Highlights on p.29)

Bayerisches Nationalmuseum, Prinzregentenstrasse 3, tel. 211 24-1. German cultural history from the Middle Ages to 19th century, with fine examples of religious art. *Tram 20; Bus 53*. Open Tuesday to Saturday 9.30am to 5pm. (See p.63)

BMW-Museum, Petuelring 130, tel. 38 95/33 07. History of BMW against a background of world events, with classic originals. *U-Bahn 3, Endstation Olympiazentrum; Bus 36, 136, 41, 43, 81, 84, 184*. Open daily 9am to 5pm. (See p.82)

Deutsches Museum, on the Isar Island, tel. 21791/2179 433. The largest technical and scientific museum in the world. *All S-Bahn lines to Isartor; Tram 18*. Open daily 9am-5pm. (See p.61)

Glyptothek, Königsplatz 3, tel. 28 61 00. Collection of classical Greek and Roman sculpture. *U-Bahn 2, Königsplatz*. Open Tuesday, Wednesday, Friday and Saturday 10am to 4.30pm, Thursday 12 to 8.30pm. (See p.81)

Münchner Stadtmuseum, Sankt-Jakobs-Platz 1, tel. 233 or 223 70. Traces city's history and development from the middle ages. *S-Bahn Marienplatz; U-Bahn Marienplatz or Sendlinger-Tor-Platz; Bus 52, 56*. Open Tuesday and Thursday 10am to 5pm, Wednesday 10am to 8.30pm. (See p.64)

Museum Mensch und Natur, in Schloss Nymphenburg, tel. 17 64 94. Museum about mankind, the earth and biological and environmental issues. *Tram 12, Bus 41*. Open daily 10am to 12.30pm and 13.30 to 4pm. (See p.86)

Städtische Galerie, Luisenstr. 33, tel. 233-0320 and 233-3200. Large collection of 19th- and 20th-century art, particularly 'Blaue Reiter' school, in the Lenbachhaus. *U-Bahn 2, Königsplatz*. Open daily except Monday, 10am to 6pm. (See p.83)

ZAM, Westenriederstrasse 26, tel. 290 41 21. Centre for unusual museums, including collections of chamber pots, pedal cars and padlocks. *S-Bahn Isartor; Tram 18, 20*. Open daily 10am to 6pm. (See p.105) with Botticelli's *Beweinung* (Lamentation) of 1490.

Three paintings by Giotto from the 14th century are *Das letzte Abendmahl* (Last Supper), *die Kreuzigung* (the crucifixion) and *Christus in der Vorhölle* (Christ in Purgatory).

Albrecht Dürer's work *Vier Apostel* (The Four Apostles), from 1526, is a noble portrayal of John with Peter, and Paul with Mark. The strips of text from Martin Luther's Bible were removed by Maximilian I as he was afraid of criticism by the Jesuits. Also by Dürer is the *Self-portrait* of 1500; although imbued with great vanity (note the Christ-like pose), it is nonetheless masterful.

His contemporary, Matthias Grünewald, displays his more down-to-earth qualities in the gentle work *Hl. Erasmus und Hl. Mauritius im Gespräch vertieft* (Conversation of St Erasmus and St Mauritius).

The Wittelsbachs' first major acquisition was Albrecht Altdorfer's *Alexanderschlacht* (1529), which shows Alexander's victory over Darius of Persia. This was a favourite of Napoleon's and hung in his apartments at St Cloud.

An early work of Leonardo da Vinci, *Maria mit Kind* (Mary with Child) was probably painted in 1473, when he was 21. It already possesses much of the serene power of his mature masterpieces.

Munich is also privileged to have in its possession one of Titian's superb late pictures, the passionately dramatic *Dornenkrönung* (Christ Crowned with Thorns), finished around 1570 when the painter was almost 90. Tintoretto regarded this painting as Titian's legacy, and he bought it for his own collection. Another great work by the Venetian artist is *Madonna mit Kind* (Madonna with child).

Raphael, whose cool, classical temperament so impressed Ludwig I, was the painter of the widely admired *Madonna Tempi* in 1507. Other works from the High Renaissance are also on display.

An amusingly coquettish picture is *Vulkan überrascht Venus und Mars* (Vulcan Surprises Venus and Mars) by

Tintoretto, in which Mars can be seen hiding under a couch, still wearing his helmet.

Anthony van Dyck's works include *Suzanna im Bade* and *Ruhe auf der Flucht* (Flight into Egypt).

Peter Paul Rubens is magnificently represented by a vast panoply of his talent, including the impressive *Höllensturz* (Descent into Hell) *Löwenjagd* (Lion Hunt) and *Töchter des Leukippos* (Daughters of Leucippus). A loving portrait of Rubens' young second wife, Hélène Fourment, in her wedding dress (1630), finds the artist in a quieter mood.

Of the many self-portraits painted by Rembrandt, one of the most interesting shows the artist as a young man of 23 in 1629. From the cycle devoted to the Passion of Christ comes a particularly gripping work, *Die Auferstehung* (The Resurrection).

Typical of the work of Frans Hals is a revealing portrait of an arrogant merchant, *Willem van Heythuysen*.

Another outstanding work is the splendid Tiepolo *Anbetung der Könige* (Adoration of the Magi), which was painted in 1753 while the artist was in Bavaria. Its lavish celebration of rich reds, golds and blues is totally appropriate to Bavaria's Baroque traditions.

If the French and Spanish Room ranks among the most popular in the museum, it may be because of Murillo's 17th-century paintings of lively young rascals. They include

Henry Moore sculptures are a small contribution to Munich's outstanding art collections.

Melonen- und Traubenesser (Melon- and Grape-eaters) and *Würfelspiel* (Game of dice).

The inspired melancholy of El Greco is evident in his *Entkleidung Christi* (Disrobing of Christ) and there's also a superb portrait of a young Spanish noble by Velázquez.

Characteristic of the rosy view of the 18th century that prevailed in France before the revolution are Fragonard's Mädchen mit Hund (girl with dog) and Bouchers *Madame de Pompadour*. The romantic sunrise by Claude Lorrain (*Seehafen bei Aufgang der Sonne*) is a typical example of his poetic landscapes, while his *Verstoßung der Hagar* is an imaginative representation of Abraham's beduin dwelling.

Artistically, Poussin's beautifully stylized *Midas und Bacchus* and *Beweinung Christi* (Lamentation for Christ) are among the best works.

Works by Canaletto, Guardi, Goya and Turner give a good overview of the painting of the 18th and early 19th centuries. Goya is represented by **58** the *Marquesa de Caballero*.

The international art of around 1800 is represented by works of David, whose *Porträt der Marquise de Sorc de Thélusson* shows the influence of the artistic interpretation of the French revolution.

Works by C.D. Friedrich, such as *Riesengebirgslandschaft mit aufsteigendem Nebel* (Sudeten mountains with rising mist, from about 1800) are typical of the early German romantics; Stieler's *Goethebildnis* (portrait of Goethe), from 1828, is a good example of Classicism.

Spitzweg's *Armer Poet* (The Poor Poet) is a humorous satire of the naive idealism of his contemporary artists.

Overbeck's *Italia und Germania* (1811-1828) is a striking example of the German Nazarene school, also known as the Lucas Brotherhood.

The French schools, the late romantics and realists, the impressionists, Cézanne, Gauguin and Van Gogh follow in quick succession. Van Gogh's *Sunflowers* (1888) is a particularly popular work, which always draws admirers.

To finish off the tour are works from around 1900. Notice the contrast between the social realism of Max Liebermann and the symbolism of the Jugendstil, represented by Gustav Klimt or Max Klinger.

RESIDENZMUSEUM

The Residenz is so huge – with 112 rooms, halls and galleries, in addition to the 10 rooms of the Schatzkammer (Treasure Chamber) – that, for guided tours, the museum is divided up into two itineraries, one offered in the morning, the other in the afternoon. Both tours include some of the more important rooms and provide a good overall impression of the Wittelsbach era, so one tour is sufficient. You can, alternatively, wander through the rooms on your own without a guide.

The museum's main entrance is on Max-Joseph-Platz (S-Bahn Marienplatz; U-Bahn 3, 4, 5, 6 Odeonsplatz; Tram 19; Bus 53). Below are some of the rooms you can visit.

Ahnengalerie (Gallery of the Ancestors). Here you can acquaint yourself with a mere 121 of the Wittelsbachs, starting with Duke Theodor, who lived around the year 700.

Antiquarium. This monumental 70m-long (225ft) Renaissance library was designed by Friedrich Sustris for Duke Albrecht V in 1558. The room takes its name from the 16th-century busts of ancient Greek and Roman leaders on display.

Porcelain Collections. This prodigious array of French, English and German porcelain includes the delicate work of Meissen, from near Dresden, as well as local pieces produced in Nymphenburg. Japanese and Chinese porcelain and superb lacquer work form part of a separate exhibit.

Grottenhof. Designed by Sustris in 1581, this is perhaps the most elegant courtyard in the Residenz, distinguished by the graceful arcade along the eastern side and by Hubert Gerhard's fine bronze Perseus fountain set in the middle. The Grottenwand, or Grotto Wall – with a fountain in an alcove – gives the courtyard its name. A statue of Mercury is flanked **59**

by Nubian slaves, fish-tailed satyrs, nymphs and parrots, and the ensemble is encrusted with many thousands of mussel, scallop and winkle shells.

Reiche Zimmer. Together these State Rooms provide the most outstanding example of Rococo décor in Germany. Cuvilliés designed them in 1729 – and his jewel among jewels was the Grüne Galerie (Green Gallery), in which you will want to linger. The Spiegelkabinett (Cabinet of Mirrors), **60** Miniaturenkabinett and Chine-

Brilliant jewels and Wittelsbach treasures on display in the Schatzkammer of the Residenz.

sisches Kabinett are equally fascinating.

Hofkapelle and Reiche Kapelle. Of these charmingly intimate chapels, the first was originally set aside for common courtiers, while the second was for the exclusive use of the Wittelsbachs.

Schatzkammer (Treasure Chamber). A separate tour is dedicated to viewing the dynasty's spectacular collection of jewellery, gold, silver, crystal and enamelware, amassed over the course of 1,000 years. One of the earliest of the Wittelsbach heirlooms is a communion goblet dating from about 890, known as the Arnulfziborium (Arnolph's Ciborium).

DEUTSCHES MUSEUM

Zweibrückenstrasse takes you to the museum (on its own little island in the Isar, S-Bahn Isartor; Tram 18) where children have all the fun – and, since we're all children, this is a wonderful opportunity to see for yourself the largest scientific and technological collection in the world. If you were to follow the lines guiding you to each and every exhibit, you would cover nearly 20 kilometres (12 miles).

If that all sounds too forbidding, relax in the knowledge that you don't, of course, have to see it all, and that displays have been laid out with marvellous attention to the comfort and enjoyment of visitors. The models, experimental machines and audio-visual effects can nearly all be operated by visitors pushing buttons, turning wheels and pulling levers. In a country that has always taken science and technology very seriously, it is reassuring to find a place where the most complex machines are, for a change, presented as monster toys for the delight and enlightenment of boys and girls, both small and large.

Setting the tone of the museum, in the courtyard you will come face to face with 'the world's first vertical take-off jet transport plane', the Dornier Do 31 of 1967. This is no model, but the actual aircraft. Now that idea on paper may not move you very much, but the machine itself turns out to be a most endearing gizmo.

The transport section brings together almost every kind of boat, from an Indian canoe, Arab *dhow* and Irish *curragh* (coracle) to a splendid velvet-seated gondola and a breathtaking 19th-century German **61**

If you need a break from art and history, pay a visit to the dynamic Deutsches Museum.

sailing ship 60m (200ft) long. Each one of the items on display here is genuine, and not a scale model. Machinery devoted to the production of energy – including windmills, watermills, a wind-turbine of 1900 from Dresden and an exquisite steampowered fire-engine of 1893 from Nuremberg – all assumes the beauty of sculpture.

Train enthusiasts will love the first German 'Lokomobil', built in 1862 and still operating, with a gentle hiss reminiscent of a domestic steam iron. British patriots may note with interest that the Germans are pleased to have on display an exact copy of 'Puffing Billy', one of the earliest English locomotives, dating from 1813. The star attraction for youngsters, however, is likely to be the model railway – complete with 204m (670ft) of tracks, 100-odd curves and a vast railway station with its shunting yard of nine parallel tracks.

The cars on display range from Karl Benz's superb 'Automobil Nummer 1' built in 1886 to an unpainted stainless-steel Porsche sports car from 1967 – still in immaculate condition after 155,000 kilometres (96,000 miles). These exhibits stand alongside the sublimely ridiculous Prunkwagen (State Coach) of Ludwig II. He had the gilded super-Rococo fairy-tale carriage designed a mere eight years before the first car. A technical note reads: '*Bremsen fehlen*' – 'No brakes'.

Other exhibits deal with printing, nuclear energy, musical instruments and astronomy. There is also a first-rate planetarium described as 'the most modern planetarium in the world' where you can take part in interactive astronomy and laser shows. You can even inspect the old wooden bridge built in the 12th century when Munich was no more than a small settlement (see p.10).

See also p.86 for details of the new Man and Nature museum in the Nymphenburger Palace – an excellent place to visit with children.

OTHER MUSEUMS

Tourists frequently neglect to visit the excellent **Bayerisches Nationalmuseum** (Bavarian National Museum) in Prinzregentenstrasse (Tram 20; Bus 53), built in 1900. The exterior traces in different architectural styles the artistic evolution of the periods exhibited inside – a Romanesque east wing, a later Renaissance western façade, a Baroque tower and, finally, a Rococo west wing. The collection provides a truly magnificent span of German cultural history from the Middle Ages to the 19th century. It emphasizes both religious and secular arts and craftsmanship.

The museum holds a number of fine Romanesque and Gothic stone carvings, wooden sculptures and paintings from churches and abbeys that have long since disappeared or been transformed. The outstanding exhibits include *Inthronisierte Maria* (Enthroned Mary) from Perugia (1200), *Hl. Katerina* (St Catherine) from Salzburg (1420) and a beautifully ornate polychrome wood piece titled **63**

Maria im Rosenhag (Mary in a Rose Bower) from Straubing (1320), showing Mary as the proudest of mothers and Jesus still a playful little boy.

The highlight for many visitors is a collection of wooden sculptures by Tilman Riemenschneider, the great Late Gothic master of Germany, in the Riemenschneider-Saal. These include some powerful statues of Mary Magdalene, St Sebastian and the Apostles, carved in about 1500.

Another Late Gothic exhibit is one of the most frightening chiming clocks you are ever likely to come across, from the Heilbronn Monastery. The implications of *tempus fugit* were hammered home to the monks by a furious figure of Death riding a frantic-looking lion.

But you should notice, too, the admirable secular exhibits, including the Augsburger Weberstube – a room decorated with the original medieval furnishings and carvings of the Augsburg Weavers' Guild, and the Stadtmodell-Saal, which holds Jakob Sandtner's intricate 16th-century scale models of Bavarian ducal cities, Munich taking pride of place beside Ingolstadt and Landshut. Finally, look for the glorious carved doors from Egid Quirin Asam's house on Sendlinger Strasse, which depict Old and New Testament scenes.

In the museum's east wing, accessible from Lerchenfeldstrasse, is the **Prähistorische Staatssammlung** (Prehistoric Museum), which is devoted to Bavarian finds from earliest Celtic times.

The **Münchner Stadtmuseum** (Municipal Museum) in St-Jakobs-Platz captures Munich's distinctive personality, and it's well worth spending an hour or two here to get an overview of the town's development since the Middle Ages (S-Bahn Marienplatz; U-Bahn Marienplatz or Sendlinger-Tor-Platz; Bus 52, 56). In the Moriskenraum is displayed the museum's main attraction: a number of jolly wooden carvings of Morris Dancers taken from the Altes Rathaus council chamber. Dated 1480, they are magnificent examples of Erasmus Grasser's Gothic style.

Hotels and Restaurants in Munich

WEST MUNICH HOTELS
and (inset) Innenstadt

Alfa

Eden Hotel Wolff

Arnulfstraße

Railway Station

Sophien-straße

Elisenstraße

Prielmayer-straße

Karlsplatz

Bayerstraße

Intercity

Häberstock

Bayerstraße

Europäischer Hof

City Hotel

Sonnenstraße

Senefelder

Mittererstraße

Schlosserstraße

Apollo

Mercure City

Daniel

Senefelderstraße

Schiller-straße

Maximilianstraße

Goethe-straße

Schwanthalerstraße

Landwehrstraße

Sparkassenstraße

Platzl

Hildegardstraße

Hofbräuhaus

Ledererstraße

Adler

Herrnstraße

Schlicker

Im Tal

Concorde

N

0   200 metres

0   200 yards

Recommended Hotels

Choosing a hotel in a city that you're not familiar with can be daunting; in this section we have selected a range of tried and trusted hotels to get you started. There are hotel booking facilities at the main tourist information offices in Munich, (see Accommodation on p.116, and Tourist Information Offices on p.135). For a short stay it is worth considering the 'Munich Key' budget packages, which are particularly good value and provide you with all you need for your visit to the city, including maps and public transport vouchers. Munich Tourist Offices can supply you with details of the scheme.

We have arranged our hotels under headings according to geographical location; Innenstadt, or Inner city; West of Karlstor, the area near the main railway station; Theresienwiese, near the Oktoberfest site and exhibition grounds; Isar, for the hotels east of the inner city near the banks of the river; and Schwabing, north of the city centre. A selection of hotels near the station and in the Innenstadt has been plotted on the map on p.65 to help you make your selection.

We have also included a small selection of hotels in the areas covered in our Excursions section, near the Starnberger See and Ludwig's follies.

The symbols below are a guide to the price of a standard double room with bathroom. Breakfast is usually extra. Many hotels in Munich supply breakfast only, no restaurant meals. These hotels are listed as B&B only. All prices are inclusive of service and tax.

❚❚❚❚	Luxury, above DM400
❚❚❚	Expensive, DM280-400
❚❚	Moderate, DM200-280
❚	Budget, below DM200

INNENSTADT

Adler I

Ledererstr. 8
Tel. (089) 23 18 80
Fax (089) 260 73 64
Extremely central location near Alter Hof and Toy Museum, with parking. 60 beds.

Bayerische Hof IIIII

Promenadepl. 2-6
Tel. (089) 21 200
Fax (089) 21 20 906
Luxury hotel in the beautiful Palais Mongelas, with full facilities including garage, bars and restaurants, roof-top garden, swimming pool, sauna and shops. Good wheelchair access. 428 rooms.

Concorde IIII

Herrnstr. 38
Tel. (089) 22 45 15
Fax (089) 22 83 282
Quiet city-centre location near the Hofbräuhaus, with several restaurants and museums nearby. Comfortably furnished with parking. 71 rooms, B&B only.

Daniel I

am Stachus, Sonnenstr. 5
Tel. (089) 55 49 45
Fax (089) 55 34 20
Comfortable, friendly hotel in a central position just off the Karls-platz, not far from the station. 75 rooms, B&B only.

Grand Hotel IIIII
Continental

Max-Joseph-Str. 5
Tel. (089) 55 15 70
Fax (089) 551 57 500
Traditional, exclusive hotel with antique furnishings, in a quiet, central location near the Maximiliensplatz. The restaurants serve international and regional specialities. Bars, banqueting and conference facilities and underground parking are available. 149 rooms.

Platzl hotel IIIII

Sparkassenstrasse 10
Tel. (089) 23 7030
Fax (089) 23 703 800
Bavarian-style hotel in the heart of Munich near the Marienplatz, with parking, restaurant and bar, conference rooms, jacuzzi, fitness room, sauna and solarium. Good wheelchair access. 272 beds.

Schlicker I-II

Tal 74
Tel. (089) 22 79 41
Fax (089) 29 60 59
Simple hotel with few facilities, but situated in the heart of Munich near the Marienplatz, with access for cars and parking available. 120 beds, B&B only.

67

WEST OF KARLSTOR

Alfa
Hirtenstr. 22
Tel. (089) 59 84 61
Fax (089) 59 23 01
Conveniently placed near the station, but in a quiet side-street location. Garage and other parking available. 77 rooms, B&B only.

Apollo
Mittererstr. 7
Tel. (089) 53 95 31
Fax (089) 53 40 33
Rooms are a good size and quiet. Bar and car park are available. 74 rooms, B&B only.

City Hotel
Schillerstr. 3a
Tel. (089) 55 80 91
Fax (089) 550 36 65
Modern hotel with air-conditioning, car park and restaurant. 65 rooms.

Eden-Hotel Wolff
Arnulfstr. 4
Tel. (089) 55 11 50
Fax (089) 55 115 555
Opposite main station, near city centre. Spacious and comfortable rooms, tasteful decoration, all windows sound-proofed. Café, bar, good restaurant serving Bavarian food, shop, banqueting halls and conference rooms available. Garage. 220 rooms.

Europäischer Hof
Bayerstr. 31
Tel. (089) 55 15 10
Fax (089) 55 15 12 22
Comfortable hotel with all windows sound-proofed, Italian restaurant, conference rooms and car park. 153 rooms.

Haberstock
Schillerstr. 4
Tel. (089) 55 78 55
Fax (089) 52 34 734
Friendly hotel opposite station, with sound-proofed windows. 116 beds, B&B only.

Intercity Hotel
Bayerstr. 10
Tel. (089) 55 85 71
Fax (089) 59 62 29
Modern, elegant hotel, decorated in alpine style, with comfortable rooms, sound-proofed windows, restaurants and bars, conference rooms and a bowling alley. Good wheelchair access. 203 rooms.

Mercure City
Senefelderstr. 9
Tel. (089) 55 13 20
Fax (089) 59 64 44
High-class hotel situated near the main station, only minutes' walk

from the exhibition grounds, with 5 conference rooms, restaurant and car park. Good wheelchair access. 167 rooms.

Senefelder Hotel

Senefelderstr. 4
Tel. (089) 55 15 40
Fax (089) 55 15 46 11
Reasonable priced central hotel, with parking. 70 rooms.

THERESIENWIESE

Arabella Westpark

Garmischer Str. 2
Tel. (089) 51 960
Fax (089) 51 96 100
Large modern hotel, near exhibition ground and U-Bahn station, with conference rooms, swimming pool, jacuzzi, sauna, restaurant and cocktail bar. Rooms for disabled and non-smokers, suitable for wheelchair users. 458 beds.

Carmen

Hansastr. 146-148
Tel. (089) 76 01 099
Fax (089) 76 05 843
Quiet hotel south-west of the city centre, a short walk from the underground station and 8 minutes from the central station. With parking, restaurant and conference rooms. 63 rooms.

Garagen-Hotel

Lindwurmstr. 20-30
Tel. (089) 53 91 66
Conveniently placed for trade fairs and Oktoberfest. Parking available. 30 beds, B&B only.

Hahn Hotel

Landsberger Str. 117
Tel. (089) 50 270 37
Fax (089) 50 45 86
Hotel decorated in the Bavarian-baroque style, with hospitable and friendly service. Conveniently placed for trade fairs, with sound-proofed windows in 40 rooms, car park and bar. 70 beds.

Nymphenburg

Nymphenburger Str. 141
Tel. (089) 18 10 86-89
Fax (089) 18 25 40
Good service in this quiet hotel, situated to the north of Theresienwiese, not far from Nymphenburg. Restaurant serving French cuisine, bar, parking. 80 beds.

Seibel

Theresienhohe 9
Tel. (089) 540 14 20
Fax (089) 54 01 42 99
Recently renovated hotel in the Bavarian style. Well situated for the trade fair and Oktoberfest grounds, with parking and sauna. 47 beds, B&B only.

69

ISAR

Admiral München ||||
Kohlstr. 9
Tel. (089) 22 66 41
Fax (089) 29 36 74
Situated on the west bank of the Isar, near the Deutsches Museum and a short walking distance from the central city sights. Views over the lovely hotel garden, well furnished rooms, some with balcony. Bar and underground car park available. 33 rooms, B&B only.

Hilton Munich City ||||
Rosenheimer Str. 15
Tel. (089) 48 04 0
Fax (089) 48 04 48 04
Near the Gasteig cultural centre, conveniently placed for direct transport to the airport. Facilities include restaurants, bar, ballrooms and conference rooms and garage. wheelchair access and facilities for disabled guests. 479 rooms.

Palace |||||
Trogerstr. 21
Tel. (089) 47 05 091
Fax (089) 47 05 090
Small luxury hotel with elegant classical furnishings and attractive garden. Situated near the Friedensengel, convenient for museums and Gasteig, with conference facilities, bar, sauna. 73 rooms.

Penta Hotel |||||
Hochstr. 3
Tel. (089) 48 030
Fax (089) 448 82 77
Opposite the Gasteig near the Isar, a large hotel with elegant modern décor and all possible facilities including air conditioning, sauna, solarium, swimming pool, hairdresser, car rental, boutiques, conference rooms and 4 restaurants. S-bahn station under the hotel. 571 rooms.

Prinzregent |||||
Ismaninger Str. 42-44
Tel. (089) 41 60 50
Fax (089) 41 605-466
Exclusive, traditionally decorated, Bavarian style hotel, in quiet location near the Isar. Close to underground station and Gasteig. Sauna, bar, parking, conference rooms, non-smoking rooms available. 66 rooms, B&B only.

SCHWABING

Astoria |
Nikolaistrasse 9
Tel. (089) 39 50 91
Fax (089) 34 14 96
Small hotel situated just off Leopoldstrasse towards the Englischer Garten. Some parking spaces available, bicycles for hire. 50 beds, B&B only.

Biederstein   I

Keferstr. 18
Tel. (089) 39 50 72
Fax (089) 34 85 11
Idyllic location on the edge of the Englischer Garten, many rooms with balcony. Garage available. 45 beds, B&B only.

Consul   I

Viktoriastr. 10
Tel. (089) 33 40 35
Fax (089) 39 92 66
Quiet location a few streets from Leopoldstrasse. Parking, pets welcome. 58 beds, B&B only.

Holiday Inn   IIII-IIIII
Crowne Plaza

Leopoldstrasse 194
Tel. (089) 38 17 90
Fax (089) 38 17 98 88
International hotel with restaurants, bars, swimming pool, sauna and solarium, parking. 6 conference rooms. 644 beds.

Hotel Hauser   I

Schellingstr. 11
Tel. (089) 28 10 06
Fax (089) 28 11 98
Small, attractive and comfortable hotel south of Schwabing, near the University and Englischer Garten, with sauna and solarium, parking. Welcomes children; cots, high chairs etc. available. 34 rooms.

International   II

Hohenzollernstr. 9
Tel. (089) 39 80 01
In the heart of Schwabing just behind Leopoldstrasse, with parking. 122 beds, B&B only.

Mercure Schwabing   I

Leopoldstrasse 120-122
Tel. (089) 390 550
Fax (089) 349 344
Situated on the main street of Schwabing. Underground parking available. 167 rooms, B&B only.

Residence   II-III

Artur-Kutscher-Platz 4
Tel. (089) 38 17 80
Fax (089) 38 178 951
In a quiet location near Englischer Garten and Münchner Freiheit. Good facilities including bar and restaurant, conference rooms, car park and indoor swimming pool. 168 rooms.

Vitalis   II

Kathi-Kobus-Str. 24
Tel. (089) 12 00 80
Fax (089) 129 83 82
Friendly hotel situated below the Olympic Stadium; the large rooms have good views over Munich. Garage and car park available. Facilities include restaurant, bistro, bar, roof garden and swimming pool. 145 beds.

71

Weinfurtner's Garden Hotel II

Leopoldstr. 132
Tel. (089) 36 80 04
Fax (089) 36 20 89
On Schwabing's main street, with hotel garden, bar and restaurant, conference rooms and parking. 345 beds, some apartments.

STARNBERGER SEE

Bayerischer Hof I

Bahnhofsplatz 12
82319 Starnberg
Tel. (08151) 2750
Fax (08151) 12190
Traditional old hotel, renovated and comfortably furnished. Roof terrace with magnificent views of the lake and Alps, beer garden and café serving local specialities. Parking available, watersports facilities nearby. Convenient for S-bahn station. 30 rooms

Dorint Hotel Leoni II

Assenbucher Str. 44
82335 Berg-Leoni
Tel. (08151) 5060
Fax (08151) 506140
A modern hotel directly on the edge of the Starnberger See, with balconies in most rooms. Swimming pool, sauna, conference facilities, 2 restaurants, beer garden and lakeside terrace. 68 rooms.

Kaiserin Elisabeth I-II

Tutzinger Str. 2-6
82340 Felafing
Tel. (08157) 1013
Fax (08157) 4939
Former residence of the Kaiserin Elisabeth in a superb location in parkland on the lakeside, with 18-hole golf course. Bar and popular restaurant with terrace, conference facilities and tennis. 74 rooms.

Marina II

Am Yachthafen, 82347 Bernried
Tel. (08151) 9320
Fax (08158) 7117
Large holiday complex of apartments and hotel rooms with balconies, on the edge of the lake. Good sports and entertainments facilities, 2 restaurants. 70 rooms.

Schloß Berg I-II

Ölschlag 9, 82335 Berg
Tel. (08151) 50101
Fax (08151) 50105
Traditional-style hotel on the edge of the Starnberger See, with all modern facilites; sauna, jacuzzi, bicycle hire, large restaurant and conference facilities. 104 rooms.

Seehof I

Bahnhofsplatz 6
82319 Starnberg
Tel. (08151) 60013
Fax (08151) 28136

Near Starnberg station, with balconies and views of lake from some rooms. Parking. 60 beds.

Simon

Bahnhofsplatz 6
82131 Gauting
Tel. (089) 8501415
Fax (089) 8501474
Next to S-bahn station with playground and facilities for children, sauna and fitness-room, free bicycle hire, lift, parking. 20 rooms.

Tutzinger Hof

Tutzinger-Hof-Platz 7
82319 Starnberg
Tel. (08151) 3081/83
Fax (08151) 28138
Old established inn, 5 minutes from S-bahn station and lake, with parking, beer garden and excellent restaurant specializing in Bavarian food and fish dishes. 38 rooms.

LUDWIG'S FOLLIES

Alte Post

Marienplatz 19
86956 Schongau
Tel. (08861) 23 200
Fax (08861) 2320 80
A popular and attractive traditional hotel on the market place in the centre of this old town, with restaurant and parking. 34 rooms with double-glazing.

Ilgen

Ilgen 2
86989 Steingaden
Tel. (08862) 12 07
Fax (08862) 12 07
Small, attractive inn, conveniently situated in this village on the B17. Restaurant with terrace. 14 rooms.

Keppeler

Hauptplatz 15
86971 Peiting
Tel. (088 61) 6201
Fax (088 61)66004
Bavarian-style family inn with restaurant, beer garden and conference room. 23 rooms.

Zum Dragoner

Ammergauer Str. 11
86971 Peiting
Tel. (08861) 6051
Fax 677 58
Established family-run hotel with sauna, skittle alley, conference facilities and good restaurant. 51 rooms with balcony.

Zum Pinzger

Am Hauptplatz
86971 Peiting
Tel. (08861) 6240
Fax 681 07
Highly recommended small hotel with attractive beer garden and popular restaurant; caters for diets. 18 comfortably furnished rooms. **73**

Recommended Restaurants

Munich has a wide range of restaurants, including Hungarian, Italian, French, Greek and other nationalities. We have tried to cover all areas of the city in our selection, but you will find many of the best restaurants in the Innenstadt or Schwabing. We have included some of the major beer halls and beer gardens in our selection as they are an important focal point of Munich life; they usually serve light meals, snacks and regional specialities. Please note that in the more expensive restaurants formal dress is expected, including a jacket and tie for men.

The following symbols correspond to the price of a 3-course meal for two people, not including wine.

▯▯▯▯	Above DM160
▯▯▯	DM120-160
▯▯	DM90-120
▯	Below DM90

INNENSTADT

Augustiner Gaststätten ▯
Neuhauser Str. 16
Tel. (089) 55 19 92 57
Bavarian beer garden, serving excellent food, including both Bavarian and international dishes, open every day till midnight.

Boettner ▯▯▯▯
Theatinerstr. 8
Tel. (089) 22 12 10
Old Munich restaurant with an excellent reputation. Specialities include lobster, oysters, caviar and other seafood. Traditional décor. Closed Saturday evening.

Berni's Nudelbrett ▯
Petersplatz 8 (1st floor)
Tel. (089) 26 44 69
Central restaurant overlooking the Viktualienmarkt, specializing in Italian pasta dishes and steaks. There is also a good selection of wines on offer. Open daily from 11am to 11pm.

Bayerischer Hof Garden Restaurant ▯▯▯
Bayerischer Hof Hotel
Promenadeplatz 2-6
Tel. (089) 212 20-993
Bavarian specialities served in the garden and on the terrace of this exclusive hotel.

Glöckl am Dom ▌

Frauenplatz 9
Tel. (089) 22 03 85
100-year old tavern, serving Bavarian specialities and one of the city's best beers. Known particularly for its Nürnberger Bratwurst.

Haxnbauer ▌▌

Am Platzl, Münzstr. 8
Tel. (089) 22 19 22
Old Bavarian tavern specializing in spit-roast meats and regional dishes. Reservations advisable.

Hofbräuhaus am Platzl ▌

Am Platzl 9
Tel. (089) 22 16 76
The famous Munich beer hall, traditional Bavarian-style, with live brass band music, serving sausages and regional specialities.

Hundskugel ▌▌

Hotterstr. 18
Tel. (089) 26 42 72
This inn claims to be Munich's oldest; serves good home-cooked Bavarian dishes and grilled meats in a friendly, relaxed atmosphere.

Hunsingers ▌▌▌

Falkenturnstr. 10
Tel. (089) 29 79 09
Highly rated restaurant specializing in fish; try the bouillabaisse. Open till 1am, closed Sunday.

India King ▌

Marienstr. 4
Tel. (089) 22 15 09
If you need a change from Bavarian fare, try this Indian restaurant which serves delicious, high-quality meals. The tandoori dishes are particularly good.

Le Gourmet Schwarzwälder ▌▌▌

Hartmannstr. 8
Tel. (089) 212 0958
Traditional old décor, imaginative, quality cuisine with French influence, by award-winning chef Otto Koch. Extensive wine list. Closed Monday and Sunday. Reservations required.

Prince Myschkin ▌

Hackenstr. 2
Tel. (089) 26 55 96
Fax (089) 26 44 96
Spacious and elegant vegetarian restaurant which serves imaginative dishes from 11am to midnight every day. Non-smoking tables available. Brunch served on Sunday from 11am to 3pm.

Zur Weiss-Blauen Rose ▌

Marienplatz 11
Tel. (089) 236 91-471
Bavarian-style cuisine. Hot meals served from 10am to 8pm every weekday.

75

AROUND KARLSPLATZ

Aubergine ▮▮▮
Maximiliansplatz 5
Tel. (089) 59 81 71
Fax (089) 550 43 53
Superb cuisine, with innovative and more traditional dishes served in elegant modern surroundings. Closed on Sunday and Monday. Reservations essential.

Augustinerkeller ▮
Arnulfstr. 52
Tel. (089) 59 43 93
Attractively shaded Bavarian-style beer garden serving Wurst and traditional regional snacks, with good beer.

Königshof ▮▮▮▮
Karlsplatz 25
Tel. (089) 551 360
Elegant restaurant serving mainly quality French cuisine, with pleasant views over Karlsplatz. Reservations required.

Mathäser Bierstadt ▮
Stachus
Tel. (089) 59 28 96
This beer hall on Karlsplatz claims to have the world's largest selection of beers. It also has live oompah music and a courtyard beer garden, and serves a range of typical Bavarian dishes.

Opus One ▮
Seidlstr. 18
Tel 55 76 81
Just north-west of the station, this restaurant serves sophisticated Californian food and wines, and a range of American-style snacks and sandwiches. Open until 10.30 to 11pm.

Trader Vic's ▮▮
Hotel Bayerischer Hof
Promenadeplatz 2-6
Tel. (089) 22 61-92
Polynesian specialities and various exotic drinks.

THERESIENWIESE

Canton ▮▮▮
Theresienstr. 49
Tel. (089) 52 21 85
Popular Chinese restaurant, with good food and service. Open 11.30am-3pm and 5.30-11.30pm.

La Fiorentina ▮▮
Goethestr. 41
Tel. (089) 53 41 85
Freshly made, good quality Italian food and Italian ambiance.

Glockenbach ▮▮▮
Kapuzinerstr. 29
Tel. (089) 53 40 43
Popular restaurant specializing in Bavarian and French-style cuisine,

with fresh fish and game. Closed Sunday and Monday. Reservations required.

Gundel III

Hungar-Hotel
Paul-Heyse Str. 24
Tel. (089) 51 49 00

One of the famous chain of Hungarian restaurants, produces quality Hungarian dishes in a friendly atmosphere.

Hackerkeller und Schäfflerstuben I

Theresienhöhe 4
Tel. (089) 50 70 04
Fax (089) 50 17 21

Bavarian beer garden serving traditional snacks, spit-roast ox and beer from the pump. Live music. Open till 1am.

Pschorrkeller I

Theresienhöhe 7
Tel. (089) 50 10 88

Typical Bavarian beer garden.

ISAR

Brasserie II

Arabellastr. 5
Bogenhausen
Tel. (089) 92 32-4433

Bistro meals and buffet, and popular Sunday brunch, in the Arabella Hotel, Bogenhausen.

Diyar Taverna I

Wörth-str. 10
Tel. (089) 448 7503

Popular Turkish restaurant serving quality food. New menu daily, reservations recommended.

El Espagnol I

Pariserstr. 46
Tel. (089) 48 84 96

Beyond the Gasteig centre, off Rosenheimer Strasse. this is a well-known, lively Spanish restaurant serving all the popular dishes.

Käferschenke III

Prinzregentstr. 73
Bogenhausen
Tel. (089) 4 16 80

Specializes in fresh fish dishes. Outdoor dining, rustic and period furnishings, closed Sunday. Reservations recommended.

Kam Yi I

Rosenheimerstr. 32
Tel. (089) 448 13 66

Popular Chinese restaurant across the road from the Gasteig Centre. Open till midnight.

La Cabana I

Tal 26
Tel. (089) 22 00 01

Steak restaurant serving quality beef and lamb steaks with a variety of seasonal salads.

Olympia ▮

Kellerstr. 29
Tel. (089) 48 80 82

Located near the Gasteig, an authentic Greek restaurant serving good country-style food. Choose your dishes from those on display in the kitchen.

Preysing Keller ▮▮▮

Innere Wiener Str. 6
Tel. (089) 481 015

Excellent modern German cuisine served in this cellar restaurant. Reservations required.

Rio ▮

Fraunhofer str. 43
Tel. (089) 201 49 93

Between Sendlinger Tor and the Reichenbach Brücke, the Rio serves Brazilian dishes and cocktails to the accompaniment of Samba music.

Rue des Halles ▮▮

Stein str. 18
Tel. (089) 48 56 75

A bistro-type restaurant serving quality French food.

Sabitzers ▮▮▮▮

Reitmorstr. 21
Tel. (089) 298584

Extravagant and unusual nouvelle cuisine, beautiful classical décor. Reservations required.

Santa Fe ▮

Balanstr. 16
Tel. (089) 48 47 36

American and American-Indian food, cocktails and American teas served among cacti in an exotic South American décor.

Tai Tung ▮▮

Prinzregentenstr. 60
(Villa Stuck)
Tel. (089) 47 11 00

Good Chinese restaurant, closed Monday.

Tofu am Isartor ▮

Herrnstr. 11
Tel. (089) 290 41 35

Vietnamese vegetarian dishes; garden open for meals in summer.

Weisses Bräuhaus ▮

Baumkirchner str. 5
Tel. (089) 431 63 81

Bavarian-style beer hall specializing in Weißbier, also the best place to go for Weisswurst, open 8.30am to midnight.

SCHWABING

Baltzer ▮▮

Volkartstr. 70, Neuhausen
Tel. (089) 12 39 19 19

Elegant, modern-style vegetarian restaurant, relaxed ambiance, specialities include vegetarian strudels. Open from 9am Sundays and holidays, from 6pm other days.

Chinesischer Turm   ▯

Englischer Garten 3
Tel. (089) 39 50 28
One of Munich's first and largest beer gardens, with traditional live oompah music, serving the typical Bavarian snacks.

Halali   ▯▯

Schönfeldstr. 22
Tel. (089) 285909
Traditional Munich restaurant serving Bavarian dishes and imaginative new German cuisine using local ingredients. Good service. Reservations recommended.

Il Gattopardo   ▯▯

Georgenstr. 67
Tel. (089) 271 65 25
Traditional Italian meals served in attractive surroundings.

Italy   ▯

Leopoldstr. 108
Tel. (089) 34 64 03
Good quality but basic Italian food, mainly pasta and pizzas.

La Piazzetta   ▯

Oskar-v.-Miller-Ring 3
Tel. (089) 28 29 90
Modern Italian restaurant in the Florentine style, just beyond the Odeonsplatz. Outdoor dining and beer garden. Closed for lunch on Saturday.

Luigi Malone's   ▯

Leopoldstr. 28a
Tel. (089) 39 50 71
American-style diner serving the usual burgers and steaks, as well as lunch specials.

Opatija   ▯

Briennerstr. 41
Tel. (089) 59 12 02
An established Balkan restaurant, serving generous portions of good food in a relaxed and friendly atmosphere.

Max-Emanuel-Brauerei   ▯

Adalbert Str. 33
Tel. (089) 271 51 58
Small beer hall serving typical Bavarian fare. Live music and lively atmosphere.

Tantris   ▯▯▯

Johann-Fichte-Str. 7
Tel. (089) 36 20 61
Fax (089) 3 61 84 69
Superb nouvelle cuisine served in this modern restaurant with its stark and startling modern décor. Outdoor dining, closed Sunday and for lunch on Monday and Saturday, reservations essential.

Werneckhof   ‖

Wernckstr. 11
Tel. (089) 39 99 36
An elegant French restaurant with
Bavarian décor, serving a range of
good, freshly cooked dishes.

STARNBERGER SEE

Andechser Hof   ‖

Tel. (08158) 1822
Bavarian-style restaurant and large
beer garden, serving quality food,
mainly local specialities.

Dorint Hotel Leoni   ‖

Assenbucher Str. 44, Berg-Leoni
Tel. (08151) 5060
A modern hotel and restaurant
with an attractive lakeside terrace.

Kaiserin Elisabeth   ‖

Tutzinger Str. 2-6, Felafing
Tel. (08157) 1013
Popular restaurant with terrace,
overlooking the park and lake.

Maximilian   ‖‖

Ostwaldstr. 16, Starnberg
Combination of new German and
Bavarian-style cuisine in elegant
surroundings.

Schloß Berg   ‖

Ölschlag 9, 82335 Berg
Tel. (08151) 50101
80 Large restaurant, lakeside terrace.

Tutzinger Hof   ‖‖

Tutzinger-Hof-Platz 7, Starnberg
Tel. (08151) 3081/83
16th-century Bavarian-style inn
with excellent restaurant specializing in Bavarian food and fish
dishes. Beer garden.

LUDWIG'S FOLLIES

Buchberger   ‖

Füssener Str. 2, Peiting
Tel. (08861) 6266
Home-killed meats, fresh Weiß-
würste available on Fridays, also
international cuisine, salad buffet.

König Ludwig   ‖‖

Kreuzweg 11, Schwangau
Tel. (08362) 81081
Excellent food, game dishes a spe-
ciality. Reservations advisable.

Zum Dragoner   ‖

Ammergauer Str. 11, Peiting
Tel. (08861) 6051
Well-known restaurant specializing in fish and game, good selection of wine.

Zum Pinzger   ‖

Am Hauptplatz, Peiting
Tel. (08861) 6240
Popular restaurant specializing in
game, grilled meat and fish, with
home-made sausages. Has a pleasant, shaded beer garden.

Maps, models and photographs on the first floor illustrate Munich's rich history. On the second floor are 20 rooms furnished colourfully in various decorative styles from the past. You'll see kitchens, living rooms and bedrooms, and examples of sumptuous rooms from the Residenz, as well as cosy bourgeois homes of the 19th century, furnished with heavy Biedermeier pieces or with the more delicate Jugendstil. Highlights include a reconstruction of a very inviting 18th-century *Weinstube* (wine tavern) and an opulent artist's studio (Makart-Zimmer).

The fashion collection illustrates the evolution of styles in a town that has long been a centre for German design. A poignant effort has been made to inject a light touch into the display of wartime fashions.

Children (and adults, too) will love the **Puppentheater-Sammlung** (Marionette Theatre Collection) situated on the third floor, one of the largest of its kind in the world. Bavaria has for many years been a traditional centre for the produc-tion of glove-puppets, shadow plays and mechanical toys.

Scholars commissioned by King Ludwig I were ordered to scout the classical world for suitable works to display in the **Glyptothek** (Sculpture Museum) on Königsplatz (U-Bahn 2, Königsplatz). Around 160 pieces found a home in the massive, Ionic-columned edifice, rebuilt after World War II. The Glyptothek glories in its great treasure – the sculpture from the gables of the Temple of Aphaia, found on the Greek island of Aegina. These well-preserved friezes have been dated to 505 BC (west gable) and 485 BC (east gable). On them are warriors with their shields, fighting to defend the island's patron goddess, smiling that rather smug Ancient Greek smile. Look out, too, for other works of major importance: the *Apollo of Tenea*, a *Medusa*, the goddess of peace *Irene* and the *Barberini Faun* (named after a 17th-century Italian family of classicists).

The valuable displays of the **Antikensammlungen** (Classical Art Collections) include a **81**

beautiful series of Greek vases and urns and, above all, the highly prized collection of Etruscan gold and silver formed by James Loeb. This German-American benefactor is known to schoolchildren through the famous Loeb's Classical Library of Greek and Latin texts.

The **BMW-Museum**, situated off the Petuel Ring Autobahn, provides a fascinating insight into the history of the Bavarian Motor Works (U-Bahn 3, Olympiazentrum terminal; Bus 36, 136, 41, 43, 81, 84, 184). On display are the cars, motorcycles and aircraft engines that made BMW famous: all the classic originals are to be found here. Officials also had the excellent idea of relating a parallel history of the world events that occurred while these technical innovations were being made.

Against a stark background, with an artful use of lighting to highlight the exhibits, contemporary history is unfolded in its political, social and cultural dimensions. Short video films are shown and vocal testimony is heard from life-sized figures of German chancellors, American presidents, and even from celebrities such as Elvis Presley and Marilyn Monroe.

One of the more unusual among Munich's museums is the **Museum für erotische Kunst** (Museum of erotic art), Odeonsplatz 8/I (U-bahn 3, 4, 5, 6). Here you can compare the various examples of erotic art from across the centuries, and from a range of different cultures.

The **Städtische Galerie** (U-Bahn 2, Königsplatz), a municipal art gallery and museum situated in the Lenbachhaus (see p.45), gives an overview of Munich painting from the Gothic period to the present day. The most important and popular collections however are those from the 19th and 20th centuries.

The villa, built in the style of the Florentine renaissance, was originally the residence of Franz von Lenbach. In 1929 it became a gallery for the famous Blaue Reiter collection, and it now holds the largest collection of Wassily Kandinsky paintings in Germany, in addition to canvases by Franz Marc, Gabriele Münter, Alexej von Jawlensky, August Macke and Paul Klee. These artists were the members of Munich's pre-World War I 'Blaue Reiter' (Blue Rider) school of painting. The name derives from a blue-and-black horseman drawn by Kandinsky for an almanac in 1912. Horses and the colour blue were also dominant features of Franz Marc's work.

Alongside these works the Lenbachhaus collections also include a number of works by Picasso, Braque, Dalí, the German Expressionists and a distinguished array of contemporary Americans.

The museum serves as a busy cultural centre, staging concerts, lectures and regular temporary exhibitions. There is a café in the grounds serving coffee and cold drinks, and on a hot summer day the lovely gardens and Mediterranean-style terrace are particularly inviting when you feel in need of a break from sightseeing.

Degenerates Forever!

Hitler's speech inaugurating the Haus der Deutschen Kunst in 1937 attacked the 'obscenities' of avant-garde art and forbade any painter to use colours that the 'normal' eye could not perceive in nature. Two exhibitions were held to distinguish so-called great German art from that designated 'degenerate art'.

The trouble was that the 'degenerate' show was far more popular, and attracted 2 million visitors, five times as many as the other exhibition. Afterwards, many of these paintings, including works by Kandinsky, Mondrian, Kokoschka and Chagall, were hidden away or sold abroad for valuable foreign currency. Back in the Haus der Kunst today, they are diplayed in the west wing of the house, alongside international paintings and sculpture from the 20th century.

Royal Retreats

Schloss Nymphenburg, now inside the ever-expanding city limits, was the Wittelsbachs' summer refuge, away from the heat of their Residenz in the city centre. This gleaming palace is set in extensive grounds with fountains, ponds and four enchanting garden pavilions – it's the perfect place to stroll and recall the *dolce farniente* of the Wittelsbach days, when they played at nymphs and shepherds here and forgot all about the worries of state. There's no U-Bahn station at the palace, but if you don't have a car for the 8-km (5-mile) ride, a No. 12 tram will take you there from the Shiedplatz U-Bahn station.

In 1662 Princess Henriette Adelaide presented to her husband his new son and heir. The birth of the child inspired the architects of the time to build both the Theatinerkirche and the Nymphenburg. The palace had modest enough beginnings as a small summer villa, but it grew over the next century as each succeeding ruler added another wing or his own little pavilion and changed the landscaping of the gardens. Max Emanuel, the little baby who was the cause of it all, grew up with the ambition of emulating Louis XIV's Versailles. While he may not have succeeded completely in this, the French armies appreciated his efforts and made Nymphenburg their headquarters in 1800.

The palace is approached by a long canal with avenues on either bank leading to a semicircle of lawns, the Schlossrondell, which is the site of the building containing the royal porcelain factory (see Shopping, p.101). In the central edifice of the palace proper are galleries of fine 18th-century stucco work and ceiling frescoes. The majestic two-storey banqueting hall, **Steiner Saal** (Stone Hall), contains several lively frescoes by Johann Baptist Zimmermann on the theme *Nymphen huldigen der Göttin Flora* (Nymphs Pay Homage to the Goddess Flora).

To the south, the first pavilion is the home of the famous **Schönheitengalerie** (Gallery of Beautiful Women). Ludwig I commissioned Joseph Stieler to paint these portraits of Munich's most beautiful young women. The ferocious-looking lady with the belt of snakes and whip in hand, the notorious Lola Móntez, was probably his mistress. She was born Mary Dolores Eliza Rosanna Gilbert, daughter of an Irish adventurer. As her mother was reputedly a Spanish countess, she went on stage as Señora Maria de los Dolores Porris y Móntez (see p.20).

The **Marstallmuseum** – a dazzling collection of state coaches used for coronations,

Relive the glamour of the Wittelsbach dynasty with a visit to the summer villa at Nymphenburg.

weddings and other royal frolics – has been installed in the south wing, in what was once the royal stables. Starting from the extravagance of Karl Albrecht's 18th-century coronation coaches, the vehicles went on to achieve a state of ornamental delirium under Ludwig II. Look out for his Nymphenschlitten (Nymph sleigh), designed for escapades in the **85**

Alps. On the first floor is the beautiful **Bäuml** collection of Nymphenburg porcelain, covering examples of the entire output from the Nymphenburg factory, from the early days in the 18th century to the 1920s. The Castle Lustheim also has a fine porcelain collection.

Also in the Nymphenburg palace is the extensive **Museum Mensch und Natur** (Man and Nature museum) opened in 1990. The exhibits successfully bring this subject to life and hold the attention of children (and adults) of all ages through the use of films, audio-visual programmes and interactive models. The museum covers a variety of topics, including an exploration of the history of the planet and of life on earth, emphasizing the variety of forms of life and the importance of their interaction. The position of man in the universe and his responsi-

F
rescos animate the walls of the magnificent banqueting hall at Schloß Nymphenburg.

bilities towards the environment are important themes, and numerous ecological topics such as land erosion, population growth and hunger in the Third World are explored.

The palace **gardens** were originally laid out in a subdued Italian style for Henriette Adelaide, but her son's taste was for the more grandiose French manner. Later, Ludwig von Sckell was brought in, landscape artist of the Englischer Garten, and the park lost some of its formality, which makes for a more relaxed stroll, but the restyling left the Baroque and Rococo pavilions a little isolated, somewhat like longstanding tenants who stayed on in a house while new owners changed all the furniture around them. Traces of the former classical geometry can be seen in the symmetry of the Schlossrondell and the rectangular Grosse Parterre directly to the west of the central edifice. The palace grounds are decorated here and there with some attractive marble statues of Greek gods by Dominikus Auliczek and others.

Off to the left lies **Amalienburg**, one of the prettiest little hunting lodges in the country. It was begun in 1734 by the same trio who worked on the State Rooms of the Residenz – architect François de Cuvilliés, sculptor Joachim Dietrich and stucco artist Johann Baptist Zimmermann. Take a wander round the rooms where the hunting dogs and rifles were kept, the Pheasant Room next to the blue-and-white, Dutch-tiled kitchen, and, above all, enjoy the brilliant silver and pastel yellow Rococo **Spiegelsaal** (Hall of Mirrors). This was originally – just imagine – the pavilion's entrance.

Continue west to find the **Badenburg** (Bath Pavilion) – fitted with Delft china fixtures that are an interior decorator's dream – and the Grosser See, a large pond dotted with islands. Overlooking it is a promontory topped by a love temple modelled after Rome's Temple of Vesta, goddess of fire.

North of the central canal with its spectacular cascade of water is another, smaller pond. On the far side of it stands the **87**

Pagodenburg, an octagonal tea pavilion with several exotic black-and-red-lacquered Chinese chambers upstairs.

The fourth of the park's pavilions is the **Magdalenenklause** (Hermitage), built for the private meditations of Max Emanuel in 1725. Inside, the dominant theme of the paintings and sculptures is penitence. Don't be surprised when you see that the building is a crumbling ruin; the cracks and flaking plaster were deliberately incorporated into the mock Romanesque and Gothic structure, and a Moorish minaret was thrown in too.

The area lying north of the park has been given over to the **Neuer Botanischer Garten** (New Botanical Gardens), entered from Menzinger Strasse. The Arboretum at the west end of the gardens has been cleverly landscaped to resemble different climatic regions of the world, complete with their appropriate flora – pine forest, Arctic tundra, heath and moorland, desert dunes, the steppes and Alpine country are here, alongside an artificial pond.

After the flamboyance of Nymphenburg, go further west (by car or No. 73 tram from the end of Menzinger Strasse) to the refreshing simplicity of **Schloss Blutenburg** – now a convent. It's particularly worth visiting for the palace chapel, of a superb Late Gothic type rare in this part of Bavaria. The three altars display splendid paintings by Jan Polack, done in 1491: the *Holy Trinity* (high altar), *Christ Enthroned* (on the left) and the *Annunciation* (to the right). On the walls are hung some beautiful polychrome wooden sculptures of the Apostles, Mary and a resurrected Christ. These figures date from around 1500.

Finish your tour in nearby Pippinger Strasse and go into **Pfarrkirche St Wolfgang** (St Wolfgang's Parish Church). A number of frescoes attributed to Polack (1479) decorate the admirably serene interior and there are also three delicately carved wooden altars from the same period. The quiet of the church is the perfect spot for meditation at the end of a long and busy day.

Excursions

To take the full measure of Munich, you must visit its hinterland, the beautiful Bavarian countryside. This is the land of picturesque lakes, little country churches and Ludwig II's crazy castles. Visitors without a car can book a place on one of the many tours that are organized by the Munich-Upper Bavaria Tourist Office (see p.136). Each tour we propose can be done easily in one day.

LUDWIG'S FOLLIES

The two Ludwig II castles situated to the south of Munich, Neuschwanstein and Linderhof, are best visited separately. Choose one, or, if you're a real fan, you could do both.

Follow the A96 and B12 to **Landsberg am Lech** (with its interesting medieval town centre), and then take the B17, the Deutsche Alpenstrasse (German Alpine Road). Stop off at Steingaden to visit the lovely **St Johann Baptist Church**, which retains much of its 12th-century Romanesque exterior.

You'll also enjoy the pleasant walk in the old cloister.

It's worth making a detour to the east to visit the magnificent **Wieskirche**, a pilgrimage church of 1754 designed by Dominikus Zimmermann. The church's ceiling is decorated

One of Europe's most famous landmarks: the fairy-tale castle of Neuschwanstein.

with a sublime fresco by his brother Johann Baptist, which depicts Christ dispensing divine mercy. In its architecture and decoration, the church is a consummate work – perfect to the last Rococo detail.

Return to the main road for the journey to the more pagan **Neuschwanstein** (follow the signs to the castle or look for signs to 'Fussen'). A visit in 1867 to the medieval castle of Wartburg, Thuringia, first fired Ludwig's imagination with a vision of the Minnesänger – the minstrels of the 12th century – and he decided to build a castle that would recapture the aura of that romantic era.

Ludwig replaced a ruined mountain retreat of his father's in the Schwangau with an extraordinary white-turreted castle. Set in the midst of a forest of firs and pines, it overlooks the gorge of Pöllat and Lake Forggen. Be sure to visit the great dreamer's throne room, and try to imagine, as did Ludwig, the minstrel contests of another age in the Sängersaal. Wagnerians will recognize the sculptural and painted allusions to *Tannhäuser*, *The Mastersingers of Nuremberg* and *Tristan and Isolde*.

While Neuschwanstein was being built, Ludwig kept an eye on its progress from the neighbouring castle of **Hohenschwangau,** just 1km (half a mile) away. This neo-Gothic building had been constructed by his father, Maximilian II. In fact, Neuschwanstein and Hohenschwangau collectively are known as 'die Königsschlösser'. Take a look at the music room, with its display of Wagner memorabilia (the composer stayed at Hohenschwangau) and Ludwig's bedroom, noted for its star-studded ceiling and the intricately carved bed.

To reach the second of Ludwig's dream castles, take the Garmisch-Partenkirchen Autobahn from Munich, turning off west to **Ettal**. Set in a gently curving valley is a lovely Benedictine monastery with a fine domed church. Stop and admire Johann Jakob Zeiller's 18th-century fresco of the life of St Benedict. Then go on to **Oberammergau**, setting for the famous ten-yearly Passion

Play, inaugurated in the plague year of 1633. In the town are preserved some very attractive 18th-century façades, painted on the houses by the so-called *Lüftlmaler* (air painter), Franz Zwinck. The best ones are on Pilatushaus and Geroldhaus.

Ludwig's favourite castle, **Linderhof**, was the embodiment of his Baroque fantasies. The palace was inspired by the Grand Trianon of Versailles, and is opulent inside and out. Quite apart from the carefully tailored landscape of pond and park, you could be excused for thinking that the whole romantic Alpine backdrop of the fabulous Graswangtal had been created from Ludwig's imagination. Only the Venus Grotto, carved out of the mountainside and forming another Wagnerian motif from *Tannhäuser*, is in fact man-made.

Graceful baroque statues and fountains capture the fantasies of Ludwig II at Linderhof.

91

THE LAKES

Ammersee (35km south-west of Munich on the A96) is a delightful place for long walks along the lake or up into the wooded hills around it. Make for the Benedictine Abbey of **Andechs** in the hills that overlook Ammersee from the east. The church was put up in the 15th century and was redecorated in the Rococo style by Johann Baptist Zimmermann, then at the peak of his career. The monastery brewery produces first-rate beer.

For **Starnberger See**, the best route is along the S-Bahn or the Garmisch-Partenkirchen Autobahn south-west. Relax in the area's quiet, rural scenery and wander along the peaceful rush-fringed shoreline. It was here that Ludwig II drowned in 1886 (see p.21) after being held at Schloss Berg, near the resort town of Starnberg.

Tegernsee (Salzburg Autobahn, Holzkirchen exit) was once a focal point of German culture, dating back to the 8th century. Its monastery held a library that, in 1500, was bigger than the one in the Vatican. The French Revolution meant secularization and the removal of the monastery's treasures to Munich. Today the Benedictine Abbey houses a beer hall, and Tegernsee ranks as a high

The beautiful old Abbey of Andechs, in idyllic surroundings overlooking Ammersee.

Worrisome Wind

Strange things can happen in Bavaria when the Föhn blows, most often in springtime. As a messenger from the Mediterranean on the other side of the Alps, this warm dry wind gusts down the mountains' northern slopes. It so clears the air that people in Munich get the optical illusion that the Alps have moved right up to the southern suburbs.

If it gives some people migraine, others claim phenomenally clear creative insights resembling a drug-induced state. An increase in violence has been observed when the Föhn blows, but these phenomena only seem to affect people in Munich, who have been subject to the conditions over several years.

centre of German social life. Join the élite of Munich society as they congregate around the lake, partake of the iodised waters at Bad Wiessee and dine out in Rottach.

Chiemsee (to the south-east of Munich on the Salzburg Autobahn) is the largest lake in Bavaria and the backdrop for Ludwig II's most ambitious castle. **Herrenchiemsee** is situated on an island, the Herreninsel, at the western end of the lake (you can take a boat out from the jetty at Stock). Ludwig started work on it in 1878, but ran out of money – and time – in 1886. Nevertheless, he made a valiant attempt at recreating the grandeur of Versailles, and the magnificent Spiegelsaal (Hall of Mirrors) can certainly bear comparison with the Galerie des Glaces. It is a homage to the king Ludwig admired most, Louis XIV.

On another island nearby is **Frauenchiemsee** (St Mary's Monastery Church), together with some charming little fishing cottages. The church's fine 13th-century frescoes only recently came to light. Chiemsee is probably the most romantic of Bavaria's resort lakes.

NORTH OF MUNICH

This excursion takes in some of the lightest and most sombre aspects of Bavaria's past. You'll probably want to start at the darker end and relax afterwards in the lighter.

Dachau (17km north-west on B304, or take the S-Bahn, Line 2) used to be known as a pretty, sleepy little village that was a favourite with painters. Visitors came for the remains of a 16th-century château and the fine 18th-century façades on many of its houses. Then, on 20 March 1933, after Hitler had been in power for a mere 48 days, Dachau was designated as the site of the first Nazi concentration camp. It was established in a disused gunpowder factory. Today, while you can still appreciate the charming town centre, you should also visit the **Concentration Camp Museum**. Follow the signs (just like one you'll see in a 1930's photo on display in the museum), to the 'Konzentrationslager'. There are also signs reading 'KZ-Concentration Camp Museum'. You can take a bus or taxi from the S-Bahn station, but you should check on the times of buses going back to the station.

The museum was built on the site of the camp by the International Dachau Committee, funded by the Bavarian state government. Discreetly, but uncompromisingly, without unnecessary pathos, exhibitions document the camp's history. You'll see photos and uniforms, and the insignia that were used to distinguish the prisoners – black for political dissidents, pink for homosexuals, yellow for Jews. Dachau was not one of the leading centres for extermination – 31,951 deaths were recorded between 1933 and 1945 – though it did serve as a detention camp for major political prisoners and as a research station for the experiments that were carried out in Auschwitz. About 100,000 inmates were interned here. In addition to the museum, you can see the original crematorium and gas chambers (labelled 'Bad' for showers) that were built but never used, as well as reconstructed prison barracks.

Chapels and a synagogue are provided for visitors' prayers.

Continue east to **Schloss Schleissheim** and re-enter the sunny Baroque world of Max Emanuel. The Neues Schloss has a glorious staircase with frescoes by Cosmas Damian Asam. Beautiful stucco work adorns banqueting halls and galleries like the Barockgalerie, containing a fine collection of 17th-century Dutch and Flemish paintings.

It is the **gardens** that are the real triumph here – a victory, for once, for the French style of landscaping – with waterfall, canals and flowerbeds by Carbonet and Dominique Girard, a disciple of the French master André Le Nôtre. At the eastern end of the gardens is **Schloss Lustheim**, a hunting lodge, just under a mile away. After admiring its superb collection of Meissen porcelain, take time out for tea.

Schloss Schleissheim is worth a visit for its wonderful formal gardens in the French style.

What to Do

Entertainment

Munich has no problem in providing entertainment – there's something here to suit every taste. First and foremost Munich is a city of **music** with its four major symphony orchestras – the Bavarian State Orchestra, Munich Philharmonic, Bavarian Radio Symphony and Graunke Symphony Orchestra. The main concerts are performed at the Gasteig Kulturzentrum, an enormous complex that incorporates several concert halls under one roof.

In summer, there are open-air concerts in the Hofgarten, brass bands strike up at the Chinese Tower in the Englischer Garten, or you can enjoy concerts in the palatial setting of Blutenburg, Nymphenburg, Schloß Dachau, or the Grosser Saal at Schleissheim. Music does not stop during the winter when church concerts are performed in the Frauenkirche, St Michael and St Peter.

Opera has been an attraction in Munich for centuries. The town vies with Bayreuth for performances of Wagner, and the works of Mozart and Richard Strauss are favourites. Though the Italians take second place, Verdi, Rossini and Donizetti are by no means neglected. The majestic Nationaltheater makes every opera evening seem like a gala. The Bavarian State Orchestra plays under the world's greatest conductors and the summer festival (*Münchner Festspiele*) in July and August attracts the very best international singers to the city. A Munich Season (*Münchner Saison*) from December to February offers the special joy of Mozart operas in the Cuvilliéstheater. In summer, open-air opera is staged in the Brunnenhof courtyard of the Residenz.

Jazz is a favourite in Munich, and American and European musicians play nightly, especially in Schwabing. You can also find jazz musicians in the Biergarten during the summer. A big summer festival is staged at Olympic Hall.

If your German is up to it, try the first-rate **theatre**. Classical and contemporary plays are performed at the Residenztheater (Max-Joseph-Platz 1) and the Schauspielhaus (Maximilianstrasse 26). The smaller theatres of Schwabing provide a more avant-garde repertoire, as does the open-air theatre at Olympiapark.

For those interested in political cabaret, Schwabing is still the place to go. Most troupes have the longevity of a butterfly, though the best-established ones are the Münchner Lach- und Schiessgesellschaft (on the corner of Haimhauser/Ursulastrasse) and the Münchner Rationaltheater (at Hesseloher Strasse 18).

Nightclubs are found in the centre of town and Schwabing, but beer halls provide the most relaxed evening entertainment.

V isit one of Munich's famous beer halls for some authentic Bavarian Blasmusik.

Calendar of Events

For the most up-to-date information on the city's festivals and arts calendar, including a current list of times and dates, ask the tourist information office for their monthly programme of events or consult the local press.

Fasching. Starts 7 January. Costumed balls and processions.

Strong Beer Festival. Week including the 19th of March. Making and sampling of special strong beers, always ending in '-ator'.

Frühlingsfest (Spring Fair). End of April. Fun fair, concerts.

Stadtgründungsfest (Foundation of the City). Weekend around the 14th of June. Fun fair.

Nymphenburger Schloßkonzerte. June/July. Open-air concerts in the grounds of Nymphenburg.

Opernfestspiele. 3 weeks in July. Variety of opera performances at Nationaltheater, Cuvilliéstheater and elsewhere.

Oktoberfest. 16 days up to the first Sunday in October. Commemorates the marriage of Ludwig I to Princess Theresa in 1810. Beer drinking, funfair, processions.

Christkindlmarkt (Christchild market). December. Market with crafts and gifts on Marienplatz and around Frauenkirche.

If you feel like a change from cultural activity try the delightful Hellabrunn Zoo (U3 underground to Thalkirchen from Marienplatz). Here, animals are grouped according to their continent of origin, and you'll see zoological curiosities such as the tarpan, a kind of horse, and the white-tailed gnu. The antics of the chimps 'working out' in their own private gym always attract an appreciative audience.

Festivals

The people of Munich always seem to have something to celebrate. More than one hundred days a year are officially given over to festivals, processions, banquets and street dances commemorating events such as the arrival of the first strong beer of the year (*Starkbierzeit*) or the departure – several centuries ago! – of this plague or that occupying army. In fact, any excuse will do.

Fasching (carnival) is almost as mad in Munich as in the Rhineland. It runs from 7 January. Some 2,500 balls are held all over town for policemen and doctors, lawyers and butchers, artists and plumbers. There are masked processions, and market women at the Viktualienmarkt have their fling at midday on Shrove Tuesday.

The biggest blow-out of all is the Oktoberfest. This began when the Crown Prince, Ludwig (later Ludwig I), celebrated his marriage to Princess Theresa in October 1810 with a horserace, to which everybody came. They came again the next year, too, and the year after, and they're still coming from all over the world.

Although the horse race has been dropped and the festivities now take place during the warmer second half of September, the blushing bride is not forgotten – the name of the site on which the Oktoberfest

Extravagant processions and free-flowing beer mark the annual Oktoberfest celebrations.

is held is Theresienwiese. Locals, however, refer to it as the 'Wies'n', which is also a nickname for the festival. During the two weeks of Oktoberfest, revelers consume gargantuan quantities of beer, toted around ten litres at a time by the hefty beermaids. This brew washes down hundreds of thousands of barbecued chickens, and the operator of a monster roasting spit boasts that he turns out up to 60 whole oxen during the festival. And to work all that off, there's the fun of the fair:

with roller-coasters, giant ferris-wheel and dodgem cars. To scare it off, visit Schichtl's age-old horror show.

Shopping

Munich is an elegant town, the capital of Germany's fashion industry, so there's no lack of chic boutiques, especially on Theatinerstrasse, Maximilianstrasse and on Schwabing's Leopoldstrasse. Munich is also the place for the world's best selection of well-tailored garments (coats, jackets and suits) made in Loden cloth, a Bavarian specialty. This waterproof wool fabric, originally developed for hunters, has kept the people of Munich warm for over a hundred years.

You may even care to try the Bavarian costume (*Tracht*). There are smart green-collared gray jackets for men or, for women, gaily coloured dirndl dresses with a full gathered skirt and fitted bodice.

German leather goods and sportswear are good buys, and Lederhosen, those slap-happy traditional shorts for Bavarians, may amuse the children.

Nymphenburg porcelain is still turned out in traditional Rococo designs. You can view pieces at the Nymphenburger Schlossrondell's factory (see p.84). Connoisseurs should be on the look-out for old Meissen or modern Rosenthal.

German-manufactured cutlery, kitchen utensils and electronic gadgets are of a very high standard and superbly designed. You might also like to consider linens, in modern or traditional designs, which are

From dirndl dresses to haute couture – there's a wealth of choice in Munich's boutiques.

renowned for their good old-fashioned quality. A great way to save on winter heating bills is to get a sumptuous duck- or goose-down *Federbett* or eiderdown – another good buy.

German binoculars and telescopes are widely appreciated and, although the competition from Japan is keen, there are **101** still many excellent cameras on the market, especially at the miniature end of the range.

Germany has always produced excellent children's toys and its industrial prowess is reflected in the intricate building sets and model trains.

The presence of so many great orchestras and musicians in Germany means that the selection of records here is probably second only to the United States. The production of musical instruments, such as the finest grand pianos, violins – even harmonicas – also enjoys a venerable reputation.

In addition to searching for bargains in the exclusive shops in the city centre, you should keep your eyes open for flea markets. They pop up all over Schwabing whenever students and artists fall behind on the rent money, but the best are the seasonal ones known as 'Auer Dult', dating back to the 14th century. These take place over eight days, three times a year (May, July and October) in the Au district (around Mariahilfplatz south of the Deutsches **102** Museum). It is clear that these markets turn up some interesting bargains from the number of city-centre antique dealers on the spot early in the morning. Just beat them to it.

Sports

The city's great boon to sports lovers was the construction of the Olympic facilities in 1972. Visitors and regulars alike can participate in the daily programme of events and training which is held at the Gesundheitspark (Health Park) of the Olympic Stadium. For information about the programme contact the Municipal Sports Office (Städtisches Sportamt, tel. 233-87 15).

The swimming pool at the Olympia Schwimmhalle can be used by anyone, in addition to eight other indoor and ten open-air pools dotted around the town. The latter all provide lawns for sunbathing. All year round, ice-skating fans congregate at the Olympic ice rink and speed-skating track.

Munich has its share of tennis courts, too: the best are at Olympiapark, in the Englischer Garten, but the most attractive of all are those at Schloss Nymphenburg.

While serious runners might want to work out at the track in the Olympic stadium, jogging and running in the Englischer

To make the most of the fresh air and the lovely scenery why not visit Bavaria by bike?

Garten is more fun, especially the stretch along the River Isar. Running in the city is also very pleasant, as long as you get out early enough (before 7.30am) to avoid the traffic. For some good exercise and lovely scenery, try cycling the 14km (9 miles) along the river path to Ismaning, or any of the bike routes throughout Munich.

There are 15 golf courses located within a circle of 20km (12 miles) around the city. On the south-west edge of town, Strasslach has excellent courses. Other courses in the Munich area include Feldafing, Olching, Worthsee and Margarethenhof am Tegernsee. Note that many golf courses are closed on Mondays.

For people who don't want to exert themselves, delightful raft trips (*Flossfahrten*) are organized on the weekends. You can drift slowly down the Isar from Wolfratshausen to Munich, while the beer flows and brass bands play.

Spectator sports are dominated by soccer, for one of the most successful teams in Europe, Bayern München (Bayer Munich), plays at the Olympic Stadium. Rowing and canoeing events are held at Schloss Schleissheim. To the east of the city centre, horseracing is held at Riem and trotting takes place at Daglfing.

Further out of Munich, you can do some serious sailing or windsurfing on the Ammersee, and on Starnberger See and Tegernsee. The local lakes and rivers also offer good fishing.

If you want to take part in deer and wild boar hunting in the Bavarian forests, apply to the German Hunting Association for a licence (Deutscher Jagdschutzverband, J Henry Strasse 26, Bonn).

Hiking is a major pastime, especially as you approach the Bavarian Alps. Just 97 kilometres from Munich, Garmisch-Partenkirchen provides guides for mountain climbing. There are plenty of peaks to tackle, including the 2963m (9,721ft) high Zugspitze.

Once in the Alps, the whole range of winter sports is at your disposal. Garmisch has, in addition to its skiing (and a very professional ski school), its own Olympic rink for skating and ice hockey. The more sedate can try curling, and for the more adventurous there is a bobsled run.

Children

Munich, complete with fairy-tale buildings, parks and gardens, and open, relaxed style, is a wonderful city for children, at any time of year and in any weather. Many of the museums listed on pages 54 to 83 are suitable for children; the **Deutsches Museum** is of particular interest (see p.61) with plenty of fascinating machines and models to play with, and hands-on exhibits for children to operate for themselves. The **Museum Mensch und Natur** (see p.86) is an excellent new museum that explores a variety of issues on the subject of man, nature and ecology, and is full of weird and wonderful exhibits which are sure to keep youngsters of all ages entertained. You could also try the **Marionette Collection** in the Stadtmuseum (see p.81); the

*Y*ou'll find plenty of attractions for adults and children alike in the idyllic Englischer Garten.

Deutsches Jagd- und Fischereimuseum (the hunting and fishing museum, see also p.33) with exhibits on wild animals, hunting techniques, weapons and trophies, and the story of fishing equipment through the ages; and the **Spielzeugmuseum** (toy museum, in the old town hall) showing examples from 200 years of toys. The **ZAM** (centre for unusual museums, see p.55) has an Easter **105**

The collection of Marionettes in the Stadtmuseum will keep children entertained on a rainy day.

Bunny Museum and also gives children the chance to drive their own car.

If the weather is too good to spend time indoors, try a visit to the Munich Zoo (Tierpark Hellabrunn). Picnicking in the Englischer Garten or taking a bike ride down the beautiful paths along the Isar River is sure to delight, or you can join the crowds cooling off in the Isar from the Prater insel, near the Maximilian Bridge.

Two wonderful theatres for children exist in Munich: the Puppentheater (Glove-puppet Theatre) in the Künstlerhaus on Lenbachplatz, and the Marionettentheater, Blumenstrasse 29a, near Sendlinger Tor. Both put on performances for children in the afternoon as well as staging marionette opera for adults in the evening.

Eating Out

Eating and drinking in Bavaria in general, and in Munich in particular, are favourite leisure pursuits. Conviviality reigns supreme, both in the high temples of gastronomy and at the long, communal tables of the *Bräuhaus* and *Gaststätte*.

Where to Eat

With its great prosperity and tradition of good living, Munich has more refined restaurants than might be expected by those who think of German cuisine as being merely heavy and unimaginative. Most of them are in Maximilianstrasse, Residenzstrasse and Theatinerstrasse, along Schwabing's Leopoldstrasse and in Prinzregentenstrasse at the southern end of the Englischer Garten. In some of the better establishments you will also find high-quality delicatessens.

Munich's growing sophistication is such nowadays that elegance – however casual – is considered to be more impor-tant than the traditional formality of ties for men or skirts for women. It's a good idea to reserve a table in advance at the smarter places. Although a service charge of 15% is already included in the bill, not many people have been known to refuse a little extra.

The niceties of dress and advance reservations are not a problem at the more popular *Gaststätte* or *Bräuhaus* – literally meaning 'brewery', but in actual fact a beer hall. These establishments usually serve full meals in addition to beer, though in the bigger halls you should make sure you sit in the dining section. All the great breweries have their own beer halls in Munich, and beer gardens too, many of them with brass bands. In the inner city, the beer halls also provide an openair *Bierkeller*. The popular beer gardens of the Englischer Garten are at the Chinese Tower, at the Hirschau and beside the Kleinhesseloher See. *Weinstuben* (taverns), less numerous in the beer country of Bavaria than in other regions of Germany, serve wine by the **107** glass rather than by the carafe or bottle, and provide meals.

In a separate category is the *Konditorei* (a café-cum-pastry shop), the bourgeois fairy-land where you can spend a whole afternoon reading the newspapers provided. This is the perfect place for a feast of pastry, ice-cream, coffee, tea and fruit juices, with even a good selection of wines. Most provide a limited selection of egg dishes, light snacks and salads.

Munich also has its quota of fast-food chains and a myriad of ethnic restaurants – the Italian, Greek and Balkan ones are particularly worth trying.

Meal Times

Lunch (*Mittagessen*) is usually served from 11.30am to 2pm, dinner (*Abendessen*) from 6.30 to 8.30pm (10.30 or 11pm in large establishments). The majority of Germans like to eat their main meal in the middle of the day, and generally prefer a lighter supper (*Abendbrot*, or 'evening bread') at night, of cold meats and cheeses, possibly eaten with a salad.

108

Breakfast (*Frühstück*)

Germans start the day with a meal that is a bit more substantial than the typical 'Continental' breakfast. The distinctive touch is the selection of cold meats – including ham, salami and liver sausage (*leberwurst*) – and cheese served with the bread. You will not find just one kind of bread on offer, but a wide variety – brown (rye with caraway seeds), as well as rich black (*pumpernickel*) and white. If you like boiled eggs, try *Eier im Glas* – two four-minute eggs served whole, already shelled, in a glass dish. And with it all comes tea, hot chocolate or coffee – stronger than the Anglo-American variety, but weaker than its French or Italian counterpart.

Soups and Starters

Bavarians specialize in excellent *Leberknödlsuppe*, a soup made with spicy dumplings of flour, bread crumbs, beef liver, onions, marjoram and garlic. *Kartoffelsuppe* contains potatoes, celery, leek and parsnip.

Other popular soups are made with beans (*Bohnensuppe*) or lentils (*Linsensuppe*), with additional pieces of sausage.

If you prefer an hors d'oeuvre, try smoked calf's tongue served with a little horseradish sauce (*Kalbszüngerl*) or pork tongue boiled with a seasoning of juniper berries, bay leaves and peppercorns, accompanied by sauerkraut (*Schweinszüngerl im Kraut*).

Bavarian Specialities

The pig and the calf dominate Bavarian main dishes, often in combination. Pork or veal can be either pot-roasted (*Kalbs*- or *Schweinebraten*) or grilled on a spit (*am Spieß*) to obtain a marvelous crackling skin. The Munich speciality is spit-roast *Schweinehaxen*, hock of pork – sold in halves or whole. Be careful when ordering, a half is a meal unto itself. The ulti-

*T*he Hofbräuhaus is worth a visit for the atmosphere as well as for the beer and roast meats.

mate delicious roast is *Spanferkel*, or suckling pig. For a change, sample the excellent game when in season – venison, hare, partridge and pheasant. Venison is often marinated until tender and served with a sauce of sweet raisins or redcurrants, or a puree of chestnuts. Try trout (*Forelle*) – this local fresh-water fish is unbeatable if boiled absolutely fresh (*blau*) – or some whitefish (*Renke*), usually fried.

Accompanying all meals is a crisp, green salad or those familiar Bavarian staples, potato and cabbage. Choose from old standards like sautéed potatoes (*Bratkartoffeln*) or try the excellent potato salad (*Kartoffelsalat*). Cabbage or *Sauerkraut* is often prepared in white wine with juniper berries, caraway seeds and cloves. Also available is the sweet-and-sour red cabbage, or *Blaukraut*, cooked with apples, raisins and white vinegar, or a good green cabbage salad (*Weisskrautsalat*).

Snacks

Given the importance of beer-drinking within Munich's social life, snacks (*Schmankerl*) are correspondingly important both to aid and abet a thirst for beer, and to keep the drinkers 'afloat', so to speak. You eat them at any time of day.

Local people enjoy sausages of all kinds as a snack food. Pork and veal join forces in the *Weisswürste* (white sausages), flavoured with pepper, parsley and onions. The best establishments – and in this case we mean those most observant of traditional standards – never serve *Weisswürste* in the afternoon. They are then no longer fresh enough for the discerning palate, which in this case is a Bavarian one. *Bratwurst*, another sausage staple, is made of pork and grilled or sautéed. The best are the little ones sent from Nuremberg. You should

*P*retzels were invented by Bavarian brewers to soak up beer – and make you thirsty for more.

Local Customs

In a *Gaststätte* or *Bräuhaus*, you'll sometimes come across a sign on one of the long tables proclaiming '*Stammtisch*'. This means the seats have been reserved for regulars – club, firm or big family. Otherwise strangers usually sit together, after a polite query as to whether one of the empty places is '*frei*'. Fellow diners usually wish each other '*Mahlzeit*' or '*Guten Appetit*'.

It may come as a surprise that each bread roll (*Semmel*) and Pretzel is charged separately; you're expected to keep a count of how many you've eaten.

also enjoy the spicy *Blutwurst* (blood sausage) or *Leberwurst* (liver sausage).

You should also be on the look-out for a delicious snack with the misleading name of *Leberkäs*. Literally, this means 'liver-cheese', but it contains neither liver nor cheese, being rather a mixture of pork, bacon and beef, spiced with nutmeg, marjoram and onions, and is eaten hot or cold. Other great snacks include: *Reiberdatschi*, or deep-fried potato pancakes; and *Obatzta*, a spicy mixture of creamy cheeses with chives, paprika, caraway seeds, salt and pepper; and thin slices of horseradish (*Radi*).

Failing any of these, you will always be able to stimulate your thirst with the salty pretzels (*Bretzel*).

Desserts

Apart from a couple of regional variations on apple cake (*Apfelkücherl*) and plum cake (*Zwetschgendatschi*), Bavarians are quite content to join the rest of the country in the national obsession for *Konditorei* pastries. Other delicious treats on offer in Bavaria are *Schwarzwälder Kirschtorte*, the cherry cake from the Black Forest and *Apfelstrudel* made in Vienna.

111

Wines

Bavaria itself stopped making good wine some centuries ago, though the restaurants in Munich offer an excellent array of Rhine and Mosel wines, mostly white. Here's a guide to the best German vintages.

The Rhine wines with the highest reputation are those of the Rheingau – the pick of the crop being *Schloss Johannisberger*, *Hattenheimer*, *Kloster Eberbacher* and *Rüdesheimer*. The next best come from the more southerly vineyards – the famous *Liebfraumilch*, *Nier-steiner*, *Domtal* and *Oppenheimer*, and next in quality are the Mittelrhein wines, coming from Bingen, Bacharach, Boppard and Oberwesel.

The Mosel wines, bottled in green glass to distinguish them from the brown Rhine bottles, enjoy a reputation for delicacy, which has developed through the fame of the *Bernkasteler*, *Piesporter* and *Zeltinger*.

Also produced in Germany is a very respectable sparkling, champagne-like wine known as *Sekt*, from the Rheingau region of Eltville and Hochheim. (This latter region provides the

Keeping It Flowing

Most of the time, there are enough big festivals to keep the beer flowing, but Munich brewers can't bear slack periods.

In the third and fourth weeks before Easter, the so-called *Starkbierzeit* (Strong-beer Time), beer festivals promote their *Märzenbier* (March Ale). After Easter comes the *Maibockzeit*, when they push the strong dark stuff. In the summer, everybody's thirsty enough not to need too much prompting.

Then comes the Oktoberfest (see p.99), the ultimate in beer festivals, when every brewery participates in a colourful parade of horse-drawn wagons. Christmas and *Fasching* (carnival) tide the brewers over till it's time again for *Märzenbier*.

English with their all-purpose term used to refer to German white wines, 'hock'.)

Beer

Bavarians endorse the old saying that there's good beer and better beer, but no bad beer. Especially not in Bavaria.

Bier vom Fass (on tap) can be ordered by the half-litre in restaurants, but elsewhere it is often only served in a one-litre tankard known as a *Masskrug* or simply *'Mass'*. Bottled beer comes in several varieties: *Export* is light and smooth; *Pils* is light and strong; and *Bock* is dark and rich.

Bavarian beer is frequently lighter than the other German beers, but it has its strong varieties, too. If you like beer dark with a slightly sweet, malty flavour, order *Dunkles*. This is not served as cold as *Helles*, the more popular light lager

brew, which is presented with an inviting mist on the glass.

Other Drinks

If you want to be refreshed, rather than stimulated, you'll find an unusually wide assortment of fruit juices, the best of them being *Johannisbeersaft* (red- or blackcurrant), *Apfelsaft* (apple), *Orangensaft* (orange) and *Traubensaft* (grape – non-alcoholic).

*I*t's more than a full-time job keeping the beer flowing in the Munich beer halls.

To Help You Order

Could I/we have a table?	**Ich hätte/Wir hätten gerne einen Tisch.**
Waiter/waitress, please!	**Ober/Fräulein, bitte.**
The check, please.	**Zahlen, bitte.**
I would like…	**Ich möchte gerne…**

English	German	English	German
beer	**ein Bier**	milk	**Milch**
bread	**etwas Brot**	mineral water	**Mineralwasser**
butter	**etwas Butter**		
cheese	**Käse**	mustard	**etwas Senf**
coffee	**einen Kaffee**	potatoes	**Kartoffeln**
dessert	**eine Nachspeise**	salad	**Salat**
eggs	**Eier**	salt	**Salz**
fish	**Fisch**	soup	**eine Suppe**
hors d'œuvre	**eine Vorspeise**	tea	**einen Tee**
ice-cream	**Eiskrem**	vegetables	**Gemüse**
meat	**Fleisch**	whipped cream	**Schlagsahne**
menu	**die Karte**	wine	**Wein**

…and Read the Menu

Apfel	apple	**Lachs**	salmon
Blumenkohl	cauliflower	**Lamm**	lamb
Braten	roast beef	**Nudeln**	noodles
Erdbeeren	strawberries	**Reis**	rice
Geselchtes	smoked meat	**Rindfleisch**	beef
Gurkensalat	cucumber salad	**Rippchen**	smoked pork chops
Hähnchen	chicken		
Jägerschnitzel	cutlet with mushroom sauce	**Schinken**	ham
		Schweinefleisch	pork
Kalbfleisch	veal		
Kraut	cabbage	**Wild**	game
Kraftbrühe	bouillon	**Wurst**	sausage
Krautwickerl	stuffed cabbage	**Zwiebeln**	onions

BLUEPRINT
for a
Perfect Trip

An A–Z Summary of Practical Information

> Listed after most main entries is an appropriate German transla-
> tion, usually in the singular, plus a number of phrases that may
> come in handy during your stay in Munich.

A

ACCOMMODATION (See also CAMPING on p.118, YOUTH
HOSTELS on p.140 and the list of Recommended Hotels starting
on p.65)

The Munich Tourist Offices provide a free multi-lingual list of accommodation in the city with full details of amenities and prices.
They also operate a hotel-booking service at the airport and at the
central railway station for a small charge, and can help with queries
(tel. 233 03 00); part of the room rate must be paid in advance.

For a wider selection, consult the *German Hotel Guide,* distributed free by the German National Tourist Board. **The Allgemeine
Deutsche Zimmerreservierung** (ADZ) operates a computer reservation system at Beethovenstrasse 61, D-60325 Frankfurt am Main,
tel. (069) 74 07 67.

In addition to hotels, there are inns (*Gasthof*) and boarding houses
(*Pension*). The tourist office can arrange for accommodation in private homes – a nice way to get to know the local people. If you are
touring Bavaria by car, look out for '*Zimmer frei*' (room to let) signs.

The Munich Tourist Office offers a special budget promotion, the
'Munich Key'. This package includes accommodation, a special
ticket for all of Munich's public transport, and reductions on admis-
sion to museums, theatres and other attractions. The Munich Key

package can be booked at the Munich Tourist Offices at the airport and central railway station, or contact the Munich Tourist Office headquarters (see TOURIST INFORMATION OFFICES on p.135).

A list of hotels and inns in Upper Bavaria is available from:

Fremdenverkehrsverband München-Oberbayern, Sonnenstrasse 10/III, D-80331 München 2, tel. (089) 59 73 47/48

Further possibilities:

Christlicher Verein Junger Männer (YMCA), Landwehrstrasse 13, 80336 München, tel. 55 21 41 0

Haus International Jugendhotel, Elisabethstrasse 87, 80797 München (Schwabing), tel. 12 00 06 0

I'd like a single room/double room.	**Ich hätte gern ein Einzelzimmer/Doppelzimmer**.
with bath/shower	**mit Bad/Dusche**
What's the rate per night/week?	**Wieviel kostet es pro Nacht/Woche?**

AIRPORT (*Flughafen*)

Airport München Franz-Josef Straus, about 30km (20 miles) east of the city centre, handles domestic and international flights. You will find banks, car-hire desks, restaurants, coffee bars, news- and souvenir-stands, a post office, hairdresser, hotel reservation desk, tourist information office and duty-free shop.

Ground transport: Taxis and suburban trains (*S-Bahn*) shuttle between the airport and the main railway station (*Hauptbahnhof*). The S-Bahn (S8) runs every 20 minutes between the airport and Pasing via the city centre, and the journey costs DM12.80. (The trains are even equipped with places for luggage!) Tickets for the S-Bahn and U-Bahn should be purchased at the ticket kiosks at stations and in the airport. The journey takes between 28 and 45 minutes; the train station is outside the airport arrival hall (look for signs for the S-Bahn).

For general airport information, tel. 975 213 13. Lufthansa (Germany's national airline) reservation desks can be reached by dialling 54 55 99.

BICYCLE HIRE (*Fahrradverleih*)

Cyclists are well catered for in Munich, with a network of bicycle-only lanes covering some 200km (125 miles) in and around the city centre. The tourist office can supply names of cycle-hire firms, tel. 233 03 00.

It's also pleasant to tour the countryside around Munich by bike. Many train and S-Bahn stations in the small outlying towns and villages provide a year-round bicycle-hire service (*Fahrrad am Bahnhof*). A list of participating stations is available at ticket counters and tourist offices. In some places, you can hire a bicycle at one station and return it to another. Suggested itineraries are indicated at stations. Railway passengers hiring bikes are entitled to a discount.

Are there bicycles for hire at this station?	**Kann man an diesem Bahnhof Fahrräder mieten?**
May I return it to another station?	**Kann ich es an einem anderen Bahnhof zurückgeben?**

CAMPING

Four major campsites are situated within the city limits:

Langwieder See, Eschenrieder Strasse 119 (north-west, along the Augsburg-Stuttgart motorway), 81249 München, open April 1 to mid-October (tel. 814 15 66).

Campingplatz **Nord-West** GmbH, Auf dem Schrederwiesen 3, 80995 München, open year-round (tel. 150 69 36).

München-**Obermenzing**, Lochhausener Strasse 59 (north-west, along the Augsburg–Stuttgart motorway), 81247 München, open mid-March to early November (tel. 811 22 35).

Campingplatz München-**Thalkirchen**, Zentralländstrasse 49
(on the Isar river, opposite the Zoo), 81379 München, open mid-
March to end of October (tel. 723 17 07).

From the end of June through August, the city of Munich runs a
campsite for young people, **Jugendlager Kapuzinerhölzl**, at Franz-
Schrank-Strasse. A tent large enough for 300 people is set up; bring a
sleeping bag and air mattress.

Sites are indicated by the international blue sign with a black tent
on a white background. Some sites give reductions to members of
the International Camping Association.

For full information about sites and facilities, consult the guides
published by the German Automobile Club **ADAC** or the German
Camping Club (**Deutscher Camping-Club – DCC**):

DCC: Mandlstrasse 28, D-80802 München 40; tel. (089) 33 40 21

If you camp off the beaten track, be sure to obtain the permission of
the proprietor or the police, and note that camping in the rest-areas
off the motorways is not permitted.

May we camp here?	**Dürfen wir hier zelten?**
Is there a campsite nearby?	**Gibt es in der Nähe einen Zeltplatz?**

CAR RENTAL (*Autovermietung*) (See also DRIVING on p.123)

You can arrange to rent a car immediately upon arrival at Munich's
airport or central railway station. Otherwise inquire at your hotel or
refer to the yellow pages of the telephone directory for addresses of
leading firms. It's usually possible to have a car delivered to your
hotel if you wish. Larger firms allow you to return cars to another
European city for an extra fee. Special weekend and weekly unlimited mileage rates are usually available. Many airlines offer fly/drive
holidays to Munich, and the German Federal Railways promote a
'Rail-and-Road' car-hire programme.

To rent a car you'll need to have held a valid driving licence for at
least half a year; the minimum age is 18. If you do not pay by credit
card you may have to pay a substantial cash deposit.

CLIMATE

Munich's climate can go to extremes – from bitter-cold in winter to hot and dry, or muggy. The dry warm wind from the south, known as *Föhn*, can result in very clear, hot, dry conditions which are wonderful for visitors. Munich's average temperatures are given below.

	J	F	M	A	M	J	J	A	S	O	N	D
Daytime ° F	34	37	48	57	64	70	73	73	68	55	45	35
Daytime ° C	1	3	9	14	18	21	23	23	20	13	7	2

Clothing. During the winter months, you'll need a heavy coat and warm clothing. In summer you should bring plenty of lightweight garments, and a bathing suit if you want to sunbathe or take a dip. A light wrap can come in handy for cool summer evenings. It may rain in spring and summer, so be prepared with a raincoat or umbrella.

At better hotels and restaurants, more formal clothes are expected, but there are few places where a tie is obligatory.

COMMUNICATIONS (See also OPENING HOURS on p.131, and TIME DIFFERENCES on p.134)

Post offices. Munich's central post office stands just opposite the main railway station, at Bahnhofplatz 1. It remains open 24 hours a day to deal with mail, telegrams and telephone calls. A fax and telex service and currency exchange desk operate from 7am to 11pm, and write-read phones are available for the hearing impaired. Most post offices are open from 8am to 6pm, Monday to Friday (till noon on Saturdays). They also handle telegrams and telephone calls.

Mail boxes are painted yellow with a black post-horn. Stamps can be purchased at yellow vending machines near mail boxes and at some tobacconists and stationers.

Poste restante (general delivery). This service is taken care of by Munich's central post office: if you have mail addressed to you c/o *Hauptpostlagernd*, it will arrive at the central post office. Be sure to take your passport or identity card when you go to collect your mail.

Telegrams/faxes. Go to a post office or phone from your hotel or any private telephone (dial 1131). Hotels often let you use their fax machine; public fax machines are available at the central post office.

Telephone. Avoid placing calls through your hotel as the fee is likely to be considerably higher than in a phone booth. Telephone booths, glass boxes with gray or yellow frames, bear a sign showing a black receiver in a yellow square (national calls) or a green square (national and international calls). Area code numbers are listed in a special telephone book. Communications within Germany and to neighbouring countries are cheaper from 6pm to 8am weekdays and all day Saturdays, Sundays and public holidays. Telephone cards for DM12 or DM50 can be purchased at the post office.

Many international phone services have access numbers inside Germany, so you can charge international calls to your phone card.

Some useful numbers:

Inquiries: domestic	**11 88**	international	**0 01 18**
Operator: domestic	**010**	international	**00 10**

A stamp for this letter/postcard, please.	**Eine Briefmarke für diesen Brief/diese Karte, bitte**.
express (special delivery)	**Eilzustellung**
airmail	**Luftpost**
registered	**Eingeschrieben**
Have you received any mail for …?	**Ist Post da für …?**
I want to send a telegram to …	**Ich möchte ein Telegramm nach … aufgeben.**
Can I use the telephone?	**Kann ich das Telefon benutzen?**
Can you get me this number in …	**Können Sie mich mit dieser Nummer in … verbinden?**
reverse-charge (collect) call	**R-Gespräch**
personal (person-to-person) call	**Gespräch mit Voranmeldung**

COMPLAINTS

If something goes wrong that you cannot take care of yourself, report the matter to the Munich tourist office, tel. 233 03 00.

In hotels and restaurants, discuss any problems with the proprietor or manager. If you are not satisfied, contact the Bayerischer Hotel- und Gaststättenverband, Türkenstrasse 7, tel. 281 600. Department stores have a special counter (*Kundendienst*) to deal with customers' complaints. If you have a problem with taxi service, call 77 30 77.

CRIME (See also EMERGENCIES on p.126 and POLICE on p.132)

Compared to most urban centres, Munich's crime rate is quite low. Nonetheless it's advisable to take all the normal precautions. Don't leave money or valuables in your car or hotel room. Lock them in the hotel safe instead. If you are robbed, report the incident to the hotel receptionist and the nearest police station. The police will provide you with a certificate to present to your insurance company, or to your consulate if your passport has been stolen.

I want to report a theft.	**Ich möchte einen Diebstahl melden**.
My handbag/wallet/ passport has been stolen.	**Meine Handtasche/ Brieftasche/mein Pass ist gestohlen worden**.

CUSTOMS (*Zoll*) and ENTRY REGULATIONS

For a stay of up to three months, a valid passport is sufficient for citizens of Australia, Canada, New Zealand, South Africa and USA. Visitors from the Irish Republic and the United Kingdom need only an identity card to enter Germany.

As Germany is part of the European Union, the free exchange of non-duty free goods for personal use is permitted between Germany, the UK and the Irish Republic (residents only). For non-European residents, and for goods bought duty-free within Europe and the EU, the restrictions on import into Germany are as follows: 200 cigarettes or 50 cigars or 250g tobacco, and 1l of spirits or 2l of wine (including fortified wines).

Restrictions for visitors from outside Europe on returning to their home country are as follows: **Australia**, 250g tobacco products and 1 litre of alcoholic beverages; **Canada**, 200 cigarettes and 50 cigars and 400g tobacco, 1.1l of liquor or wine or 8.5l of beer; **USA**, 200 cigarettes and 100 cigars and a reasonable amount of tobacco, 1 US quart of alcoholic beverages.

Currency restrictions. There are no restrictions on the import or export of marks or any other currency.

I've nothing to declare.	**Ich habe nichts zu verzollen**.
It's for personal use.	**Es ist für meinen persönlichen Gebrauch**.

DRIVING IN MUNICH

To bring your car into Germany you will need: a national (or international for those coming from the USA, Australia, South Africa) driving licence; car registration papers; a national identity car sticker; a red warning triangle in case of breakdown; and a first-aid kit.

Insurance. Third-party insurance is compulsory. Visitors have to present their international insurance certificate (Green Card) or take out third-party insurance at the German border. For EU visitors, the green card is no longer compulsory but is strongly recommended.

Seat belts are obligatory for front-seat **and** back-seat passengers if the car is so equipped. If you don't wear them, insurance companies will reduce compensation in the event of an accident.

Driving conditions. Traffic jams, a lack of parking space, pedestrian areas and one-way streets all make driving in Munich a frustrating experience. It's far better to get around town by the public transport system, which is excellent – the tourist office provides a brochure listing points of interest and detailing how to get there by bus or underground. Bear in mind that bottlenecks form on major approach roads into Munich at the beginning and end of peak holiday periods. **123**

Drive on the right, pass on the left. On the *Autobahn* (motorway, expressway) passing another vehicle on the right is prohibited; cars with caravans (trailers) are not allowed to overtake on certain stretches (watch for signs); and should police or emergency vehicles need to pass through a traffic jam (*Stau*), cars in the right lane must keep close to the right, and those in the left lane close to the left, thereby opening a passageway down the middle.

In the absence of traffic lights, stop or yield signs, vehicles coming from the right have priority at intersections, unless otherwise indicated. At roundabouts (traffic circles) approaching cars must give way to traffic already in mid-stream, unless otherwise indicated. Trams must be passed on the right and never at a stop (unless there's a traffic island).

At dusk, and in case of bad visibility, headlights or dipped headlights must be used; driving with parking lights only is forbidden, even in built-up areas.

Speed limits. The speed limit is 100kph (62mph) on all open roads except for motorways and dual carriageways (divided highways), where there's no limit unless otherwise indicated (the suggested maximum speed is 130kph or 81mph). In town, the limit is 50kph (31mph). Cars towing caravans may not exceed 80kph (50mph).

Traffic police (see also POLICE on p.132) may confiscate the car keys of persons they consider unfit to drive. Drinking and driving is a very serious offence in Germany. The permissible level of alcohol in the blood is 0.8 per mille (millilitres), or about two glasses of beer. Be careful, too, to stay within speed limits; the police are getting more and more strict, and radar is used both inside and out of towns.

Breakdowns. In the event of a breakdown on the *Autobahn* and other important roads, use one of the emergency telephones located every second kilometre (the direction of the nearest one is indicated by a small arrow on the reflector poles at the roadside). Ask for *Strassenwacht,* run jointly by the two German automobile clubs ADAC and AvD. Assistance is free; towing and spare parts have to be paid for. For round-the-clock breakdown service, call **1 92 11**.

Fuel and oil (*Benzin; Öl*). Service stations are everywhere, many of them self-service. It's usual to tip attendants for any extra attention.

Fluid measures

Road signs. Most road signs employed in Germany are international pictographs, but here are some written ones you might come across:

One-way street	**Einbahnstrasse**
Get into lane	**Einordnen**
Pedestrians	**Fussgänger**
Short-term parking	**Kurzparkzone**
Keep left	**Links fahren**
No parking	**Parken verboten**
Road works (Men working)	**Strassenarbeiten**
Diversion (Detour)	**Umleitung**
Caution	**Vorsicht**
(Internationaler) Führerschein	(International) Driving Licence
Kraftfahrzeugpapiere	Car Registration Papers
Grüne Karte	Green Card
Wo ist der nächste Parkplatz?	Where's the nearest car park?
Bitte volltanken.	Full tank, please.
Super/bleifreies Benzin/Diesel	Super/lead-free/diesel
Kontrollieren Sie bitte das Öl/die Reifen/die Batterie.	Check the oil/tires/battery, please.
Ich habe eine Panne.	I've had a breakdown.
Es ist ein Unfall passiert.	There's been an accident.

125

ELECTRIC CURRENT

Germany has 220-volt, 50-cycle AC. Plugs are the standard continental type for which British and North American appliances need an adaptor.

EMBASSIES and CONSULATES (*Konsulat*)

Canada	Tal 29, Munich 2, tel. 22 26 61
Irish Republic	Mauerkircherstrasse 1a, Munich 80, tel. 98 57 23/25
South Africa	Sendlinger-Tor-Platz 5, Munich 2, tel. 260 50 81
United Kingdom	Burkleinstrasse 10, Munich 22, tel. 21 10 90
USA	Königinstrasse 5, Munich 22, tel. 2 88 81

EMERGENCIES (See also EMBASSIES AND CONSULATES above, DRIVING on p.123, MEDICAL CARE on p.129 or POLICE on p.132)

Emergency telephone numbers:

Police:	**110**
Fire:	**112**
Ambulance:	**19222**
Medical Emergency Service:	**557755**

If you don't speak German, try English, or ask the first person you see to help you call.

There is a special helpline you can call for consultation on drugs, tel. **223 22844**, and an emergency helpline for victims of sexual violence (including rape), tel. **76 37 37**.

Please, can you place an emergency call for me to the…	**Würden Sie bitte … für mich anrufen?**
police/fire brigade/hospital	**die Polizei/die Feuerwehr/das Krankenhaus**

GAY and LESBIAN TRAVELLERS
(see also WOMEN on p.140)

Munich has an open atmosphere and is very accepting of all lifestyles. In particular, there is an area around the theater district called Görtnerplatz where there are many gay restaurants and clubs.

Information Centre for Men, Landwehrstr. 85/1, tel. 543 9556

Counselling for Lesbians, tel. 725 42 72 (English-speaking service available)

GUIDES and TOURS
The tourist office will put you in touch with qualified guides and interpreters if you want a personally conducted tour or if you need linguistic assistance. City sightseeing tours by bus start from opposite the main entrance of the central railway station, in front of the Hertie department store. Daily excursions by coach to outlying towns and villages are also organized; inquire at the tourist office for details, or at the Panorama Tours office, Arnulfstrasse 8, 80335 München.

LANGUAGE (see also USEFUL EXPRESSIONS inside front cover).
About one-third of the Munich population speaks a form of Bavarian dialect. Real Bavarian is difficult to understand, even for the many northern Germans who live in Munich; but Bavarians can often be persuaded to speak something closer to High ('standard') German. English is widely understood and spoken, and most of the larger shops have English-speaking staff, but don't take it for granted.

   The Berlitz GERMAN PHRASE BOOK AND DICTIONARY covers most situations you are likely to meet, and the GERMAN-ENGLISH/ENGLISH-GERMAN POCKET DICTIONARY contains a menu-reader supplement.

Do you speak English?   **Sprechen Sie Englisch?**   **127**

LOST PROPERTY

Munich's general lost-property office (*Fundbüro*) is at Arnulfstrasse 31 (tel. 12 408-0). For property lost at or near the airport, call 92 110.

For property lost on trains, contact the *Fundbüro* at the central railway station (tel. 128 66 64), if it is within three days of the loss. Otherwise, contact the main lost-property offices of the Bundesbahn, at Landsbergerstr. 472; tel. 128 58 59. The S-Bahn lost-property office is at the east railway station (*Ostbahnhof*), tel. 12 88 4.

For anything lost in a post office or telephone call box, enquire at the post office, Arnulfstrasse 195 (tel. 12 22 1).

I've lost my wallet/my bag/my passport.	**Ich habe meine Brieftasche/meine Tasche/meinen Pass verloren**.

MEDIA

Newspapers and Magazines (*Zeitung*; *Zeitschrift*). Major British, American and continental newspapers and magazines are on sale at newsagents in the city centre, as well as at larger hotels, the central railway station and the airport.

A monthly guide to forthcoming events (*Monatsprogramm*) is available at the tourist office, hotels and news-stands. A comprehensive monthly bulletin of English speaking events, *Eyes and Ears*, is available from tourist offices, or fax/tel. (089) 502 9261. There is an English bookshop in Schellingstrasse, near the university.

Have you any English-language newspapers?	**Haben Sie Zeitungen in englischer Sprache?**

Radio and TV (*Radio*; *Fernsehen*). You can easily pick up the BBC World Service, American Forces Network (AFN) or the Voice of America. The Bavarian Radio Service (*Bayerischer Rundfunk*) has the news daily in English. There are two national television channels – ARD (Channel One) and ZDF (Channel Two) – a regional station,

Drittes Programm, and numerous private channels. Films are sometimes shown in the original English version, and a news bulletin is relayed in English once a week. Many hotels carry CNN, NBC Super Channel and other English-language channels.

MEDICAL CARE (See also EMERGENCIES on p.126)

If you already have private medical insurance, find out if you are covered for medical treatment in Germany. Visitors who are not covered can take out a short-term holiday policy before setting out.

Citizens of European Union countries are elligible for free medical treatment, and should obtain the requisite form from their Health and Social Security Office. However it is still advisable to take out holiday insurance; a reputable policy will provide far more comprehensive coverage in the case of serious illness or accident.

In an emergency call for an ambulance (**19 222**), or contact the medical emergency service staff (tel. **55 86 61**). If you require medical attention you can contact the American or British consulates for a list of English-speaking doctors and dentists.

Pharmacies are open during normal shopping hours. At night, on Sundays and holidays, all chemists display the address of the nearest one open. For the Pharmacy emergency service call **59 44 75**.

No vaccinations are required for entry to Germany.

Where's the nearest (all-night) pharmacy?	**Wo ist die nächste diensthabende Apotheke?**
I need a doctor/dentist.	**Ich brauche einen Arzt/Zahnarzt.**
I have a pain here.	**Ich habe hier Schmerzen.**
stomach ache	**Magenschmerzen**
headache	**Kopfschmerzen**
a fever	**Fieber**
medical emergency service	**Ärztlicher Notdienst**
ambulance	**Rettungsdienst**
hospital	**Krankenhaus**

MONEY MATTERS
(See also CUSTOMS AND ENTRY FORMALITIES on p.122)

Currency Germany's monetary unit is the *Deutsche Mark* (*DM*). The mark is divided into 100 *Pfennig* (*Pf*).
Coins: 1, 2, 5, 10 and 50 Pf. and DM 1, 2, 5 and 10.
Notes: DM 5, 10, 20, 50, 100, 500 and 1,000.

Banks and currency exchange. Foreign currency can be changed at ordinary banks (*Bank*), savings banks (*Sparkasse*) and currency exchange offices (*Wechselstube*). It can also be changed at hotels, travel agencies and Munich's central post office, but rates are not as good. Money can be changed at the central railway station from 6am to 11pm every day. Always take your passport with you to change money or traveller's cheques.

Credit cards are accepted in most major hotels and many restaurants, shops and major service stations. They are also useful for obtaining cash from cash dispenser machines.

Traveller's cheques and eurocheques are welcome almost everywhere. Eurocheques are particularly widely used.

I want to change some pounds/dollars.	**Ich möchte Pfund/Dollars wechseln**.
Do you accept traveller's cheques?	**Nehmen Sie Reiseschecks?**
Can I pay with this credit card?	**Kann ich mit dieser Kreditkarte zahlen?**

PLANNING YOUR BUDGET
To give you an idea of what to expect, here's a list of average prices in marks (DM). They can only be approximate, however, as inflation creeps relentlessly up.

Airport transfer. S-Bahn line 8 to Central Train Station (Hauptbahnhof): DM12.80; taxi DM90.

Baby-sitters. DM15 per hour.

130 **Camping**. DM25-30 for two with car and tent or caravan (trailer).

Car rental. Some average examples include a *Ford Escort* or *Opel Kadett L*, DM132 per day, DM0,89 per kilometre, DM 994 per week with unlimited mileage; *BMW 316* DM127 per day, DM1,27 per km, DM1,603 per week with unlimited mileage. Tax included.

Cigarettes. DM4,20 per pack.

Entertainment. Cinema DM9-12, theatre DM25-45, nightclub usually free, but you may have to buy a specified number of drinks.

Hotels (double room per night). Luxury class DM300-792, first class DM250-450, medium class DM180-370, budget class DM120-200. *Boarding house* DM80-150.

Meals and drinks. Continental breakfast DM10 (usually included in tariff), lunch or dinner DM25-50, bottle of wine (German) DM30-40, beer (small) DM5, soft drinks (small) DM3, coffee DM4-6.

Museums. DM3-8.

Shopping bag. 1kg of bread DM6.5, 250g of butter DM 2.70, 6 eggs DM1.80, 1kg of hamburger meat DM25, 100g of instant coffee DM6.50, ½ litre of beer DM1.20, 1 litre of soft drink DM1.20

MVV city transport. Day ticket, adults DM10, children DM3, inner city or suburbs, DM20 or DM5 for whole network. Single ticket DM3.20 per zone, 12-strip ticket DM15. Children's tickets; DM1.40 for 1-2 zones, DM2.80 for more than 2 zones, DM8 for 8-strip ticket.

Taxis. DM3.90, plus DM2.20 per km within centre of Munich.

Youth hostels. Youth hostel (six-bed rooms) DM20-50 per person, breakfast included. Single rooms about DM50.

OPENING HOURS (See also Public Holidays on p.133)

Banks usually open from 8.15am to 12.30pm and 1.45 to 3.30pm, Monday to Friday (Thursday until 5.30pm). Some bigger banks in the city centre remain open during the lunch hour. Banks at the airport operate daily from about 7am till around 9pm. Transactions can also be made at the central railway station daily from 6am to 11pm. **131**

Museum hours vary, but are usually from 9am to 4.30 or 5pm. Most museums close on Mondays. (See p.55 for further details.)

Restaurants in the city centre often stay open all day. Breakfast is until 10am, lunch from noon to 2.30pm and dinner from 6 to 11pm.

Shops generally open from 8.30 or 9am to 6.30pm, Monday to Friday, till 2pm (some till 12.30) on Saturdays (until 6 pm on the first Saturday of the month). On Thursdays, shops are open till 8.30pm. Shops outside the city centre usually close between 1 and 3pm.

P ━━━━━━━━━━━━━━━━━━━━━━━━━━━━━━━━━

PHOTOGRAPHY

Some of the world's best cameras come from Germany, so you may want to get equipped here. All brands of film are available. Developing usually takes 1-2 days; some shops provide overnight service.

Most modern security machines will not ruin your film; if in doubt ask, or pass films through separately.

Videos in Germany use the PAL system (not NTSC), so make sure your system is compatible with any videos you buy. You can get videos copied from PAL to NTSC in Munich or when you get home.

I'd like a roll of film.	**Ich hätte gern einen Film**.
black-and-white film/colour film	**Schwarzweissfilm/Farbfilm**
How long will it take to develop this film?	**Wie lange dauert das Entwickeln?**

POLICE (*Polizei*) (See also EMERGENCIES, p.126)

Germany's police wear green uniforms. You'll see them on white motorcycles or in green-and-white cars. Street parking in towns is supervised by police officers in dark-blue uniforms. If you are fined, they have the right to ask you to pay on the spot.

The police emergency number is 110; the Fire Department is 112. Munich's central police station (*Polizeipräsidium*) is at Ettstrasse 2.

| Where's the nearest police station? | **Wo ist die nächste Polizeiwache?** |

PUBLIC HOLIDAYS (*Feiertag*)

On public holidays, shops, banks, offices and many restaurants are closed. If a holiday falls on a Thursday, it may turn into a long week-end. On December 24 and 31, shops open till midday. Most restaurants, theatres, cinemas and concert halls close on Christmas Eve.

Fixed Holidays:

Jan 1	*Neujahr*	New Year's Day
Jan 6	*Heilige Drei Könige*	Epiphany
May 1	*Tag der Arbeit*	Labour Day
Aug 15	*Mariä Himmelfahrt*	Assumption Day
Oct 3	*Tag der Deutschen Einheit*	Day of National Unity
Nov 1	*Allerheiligen*	All Saints' Day
Dec 25-6	*Weihnachten*	Christmas

Movable Holidays:

Karfreitag	Good Friday
Ostermontag	Easter Monday
Christi Himmelfahrt	Ascension Day
Pfingstmontag	Whit Monday
Fronleichnam	Corpus Christi
Buss- und Bettag	Day of Repentance (3rd Wed in Nov)

R

RELIGION

Almost half of the Munich population are Roman Catholic and about one-third Protestant. There is also a large Jewish community.

Several church services are held in English for different denominations, such as: St Bonifaz, Karlstrasse; Kreuzkirche, Kreuzstrasse (Roman Catholic) and Seybothstrasse 4 (Anglican-Episcopal). For times of these – and other – services, refer to the monthly guide *Monatsprogramm*, or call 11 57.

TIME DIFFERENCES

Germany follows Central European Time (GMT + 1). In summer, the clock is put one hour ahead (GMT + 2):

New York	London	**Munich**	Jo'burg	Sydney	Auckland
6am	11am	**noon**	noon	8pm	10pm

What time is it, please?   **Wie spät ist es, bitte?**

TIPPING

Since a service charge is normally included in hotel and restaurant bills, tipping is not obligatory but is widely practised. It's appropriate to give something extra to bellboys, hat-check attendants for their services. Below are some suggestions as to how much to leave.

Porter, per bag	DM1
Maid, per week	DM5-10
Lavatory attendant	DM0.50-1
Waiter	optional (round off)
Taxi driver	round off
Hairdresser/Barber	10-15%
Tourist guide	10%

TOILETS

Public toilets are easily found: museums, all restaurants, bars, cafés, large stores, airports and railway stations provide facilities. If there's an attendant, and hand towels and soap are offered, you should leave a small tip. Always have several 10-Pfennig coins ready in case the door has a slot machine.

Toilets may be labeled with symbols of a man or a woman or the initials *W. C.* Otherwise *Herren* (Gentlemen) and *Damen* (Ladies) or a double zero (00) sign are indicated.

134 Where are the toilets, please?   **Wo sind die Toiletten, bitte?**

TOURIST INFORMATION OFFICES

The German National Tourist Board – Deutsche Zentrale für Tourismus (DZT) – can inform you about when to go, where to stay and what to see in Munich:

DZT, Beethovenstrasse 69, D-60325 Frankfurt am Main,
tel. (069) 7 57 20

The national tourist organization also maintains offices in many countries throughout the world:

Canada	175 Bloor Street East, North Tower, Suite 604, Toronto, Ont. M4W 3R8, tel. (416) 968-1570
United Kingdom	Nightingale House, 65 Curzon Street, London W1Y, tel. (071) 495 3990
USA	122 East 42nd Street, New York, NY 10168, tel. (212) 661-37200
	11766 Wilshire Boulevard, Suite 750, Los Angeles, CA 90025, tel. (310) 575 9799

Munich Tourist Offices are situated in the arrival hall of the airport (tel. 2 39 11, open 8.30am to 10pm Monday to Saturday, 1 to 9pm Sundays) and near the Bayerstrasse exit of the central railway station (tel. 23 91 256, open 8am to 11pm). Address enquiries to:

Fremdenverkehrsamt München, Postfach, 80313 Munich 2;
tel. (089) 23 33 02 33.

Munich Tourist offices Offer a hotel booking service for a small fee. The official *Monatsprogramm* of events is on sale there, as are the 24-hour tickets for unlimited tram, bus, U-Bahm and S-Bahn trips.

You can also listen to recorded information in English: for museums and galleries tel. 23 91 62; palaces and sights tel. 23 91 72.

For information about Upper Bavaria, contact the Munich-Upper Bavaria Tourist Association at the following address:

Fremdenverkehrsverband München-Oberbayern, Sonnenstrasse 10/III, 80331 Munich 2; tel. (089) 59 73 47/48.

TRANSPORT

Munich is served by an efficient network of buses, trams, U-Bahn (underground railway) and S-Bahn (suburban railway, a part of the German Federal Railways). The U- and S-Bahn serve the city centre, while the S-Bahn goes out to suburbs and the surrounding country-side. All forms of public transport operate from about 5am to 1am daily. Free maps and information are available at the tourist offices.

Tickets are interchangeable between U-Bahn, S-Bahn, buses and trams, and entitle you to free transfers for up to two hours so long as you travel in the same direction. Buy your tickets from the big blue vending machines at U- and S-Bahn stations (or on buses and at tram stops, hotels, tobacconists, newsagents and stationers that display a white 'K'). Vending machines are marked *Einzelfahrkarte* (single ticket) or *Streifenkarte* (strip ticket). The strip tickets work out cheaper if you intend to make several trips. Be sure to cancel tickets in the blue cancelling machines positioned at platform entrances and in buses and trams; if you have a strip ticket you need to cancel **two** strips per zone travelled (children cancel only one strip per zone).

Make sure you keep your ticket handy while you are using the public transit system, in case of spot checks.

Munich Transport (**Münchner Verkehrs-Verbund – MVV**) also offer reduced-price 24-hour tickets which can be used throughout the metropolitan area. They are sold by machines marked *24-Stunden-Karte* and at the tourist offices, and are available for the inner zone, the outer zone, or the entire network. After 9am weekdays, and all day at weekends, one 24-hour ticket enables 5 people (only 2 over 18) to travel together within the specified zone.

Taxis. Munich taxis are beige in colour. Catch one at a rank, or hail a driver on the streets. During rush hour, it is wise to book in advance, through your hotel receptionist or by phoning 21 61 01 or 194 10.

There is a service catering for women only, but you should make sure you book your cab reasonably well in advance; tel. 755 85 37.

Inter-city bus services. Rural areas are served by the Federal Railways (*Bundesbahn*) buses and the Federal Post Office (*Bundespost*) buses, as well as local companies. In Munich, the bus terminal is in

Arnulfstrasse, in the front of Starnberg Station (on the north side of the central railway station).

Trains. Deutsche Bundesbahn trains are extremely comfortable and fast, as well as punctual. EC (*Euro-City*) are international trains; IR (*Inter-Region*) trains run every hour between major cities; FD (*Fern-Express*) are intermediate- to long-distance trains with a supplement on journeys of less than 50km (30 miles); D (*Schnellzug*, or *D-Zug*) are intermediate- to long-distance trains; E (*Eilzug*) trains make local stops; and *Nahverkehrszug* are local trains, stopping at all stations.

Reduced-price offers and bargain tickets are available, including: *Eurailpasses* (rover tickets covering most of western Europe); the *Freedom Pass* available for people under 26 years of age (for travel on any 3, 5 or 10 days within one month, in Germany and 24 other countries); an *Inter-Rail* card (one month of unlimited 2nd-class rail travel on all participating European railways).

Visitors from the UK and Ireland only can buy *Regional Passes* for a given area (contact DER Travel Service, London, tel. 071 290 1111). The pass allows five or ten days' unlimited travel on regional rail services, including Munich's S-bahn network.

Children under 4 travel free, from 4 to 11 inclusive, half price.

For further details, ask at travel agencies, German National Tourist offices in your home country, or DB railway offices.

Hitch-hiking. This is forbidden only on the *Autobahn*. However, if you try thumbing a lift, you'll be lucky if anyone stops for you.

Car-share groups. Some associations arrange inter-city trips (*Mitfahrgelegenheiten*); try the following addresses:

Mitfahrzentrale, Lämmerstr. 4, tel. 59 45 61

Mitfahrcenter, Klenzestr. 57b, tel. 201 50 89

Frauenmitfahrcenter (women only), Klenzestr. 57b, tel. 201 65 10.

There are fixed-price tickets for the journeys, according to the distance, and for a small fee, you can also have insurance cover.

When's the next bus/train to …?	**Wann fährt der nächste Bus/Zug nach…?**

I want a ticket to …	**Ich möchte eine Fahrkarte nach…**
single (one-way)	**einfach**
return (round-trip)	**hin und zurück**
first/second class	**erste/zweite Klasse**

TRAVELLERS WITH DISABILITIES

Munich is a very accessible city, with most large hotels, museums, public transport equipped with ramps, elevators and special access. It's advisable to check at smaller places before you go. A special guidebook, *Münchener Stadtführer fur Behinderte*, is available (in German) for 10 DM (Tel. 089 21 170).

In the hotel section of this guide we have noted which hotels have particularly good facilities or special rooms for wheelchair users. Contact the hotel for more detailed information.

City guides are available to accompany visitors with disabilities; call 356 88 08 Tuesday and Thursday 6 to 8pm.

Munich's central post office, opposite the station, has write-read phones available for the hearing-impaired from 7am to 11pm.

TRAVELLING TO MUNICH (see also AIRPORTS on p.117)

A good travel agent can give you up-to-date information on the wide range of fares, package holidays or short breaks currently available.

By air. Flughafen München Franz Josef Strauss is served by many European and about 90 intercontinental flights a day. However, the main airport for transatlantic flights is still Frankfurt, from where there are several flights a day to Munich. Average journey time from London to Munich is 1½ hours, from New York 9 hours.

By car. Munich can be reached by motorway (expressway) from nearly anywhere in Europe (Brussels–Munich 815km/505 miles, Basel 394km/244 miles, Hamburg 795km/493 miles).

By coach. Tour operators in Germany and abroad offer coach tours to Munich all year round. Seats must be booked in advance. London to Munich direct takes approximately 24 hours.

By rail. Information on trains and reduced-price tickets is on pp.124-125. There are numerous trains daily from London to Munich via Dover and Ostend, a journey of 17 hours. The day-service via Harwich and the Hook of Holland (20 hours) is direct, but passengers on the night train must change in Cologne. Through the summer months there's a *Train Auto Couchettes* from Paris to Munich. Seats or sleepers should be booked well in advance.

WATER (*Wasser*)

It is perfectly safe to drink the tap water in Germany; only rarely will you see the sign '*Kein Trinkwasser*' (which means 'not drinking water', usually at public squares and in trains). If you order water in restaurants you will automatically be served fizzy mineral water. If this is not what you want you should order *stilles Mineralwasser* (natural Mineral water).

WEIGHTS and MEASURES (see also p.125)

Length

Temperature

Weight

WOMEN (see also EMERGENCIES on p.126, GAY AND LESBIAN TRAVELLERS on p.127 and TRANSPORT on pp.137 and 138)

An extraordinary number and variety of organizations in Munich cater specifically for women; there is a full listing in Munich's *Monatsprogramm*. There are also several organizations specifically for English speaking women, listed in the English language bulletin *Eyes and Ears* (see MEDIA on p.128). Check the opening times of the following organizations before you visit.

24-hour help and advice for women: 354 830, 354 83 11

Women-only, guarded **car parks**: Rosenheimer Str. 5, open 8am to 12am, St Jakobs Platz, Oberanger 35-37, open 24 hours.

Frauenkulturhaus (women's cultural centre), Richard Strauss Str. 21, tel. 470 52 12.

Frauentreffpunkt Neuperlach (Meeting point, café) Oskar Maria Graf Ring 20/22, tel. 670 64 63.

Lillemor's Frauenbuchladen (Women's bookshop), Arcisstr. 57, tel. 272 12 05.

Multi-lingual **babysitter** service, tel. 22 92 91.

YOUTH HOSTELS

If you are planning to make extensive use of youth hostels during your stay in Munich, obtain an international membership card from your national youth hostel association. For full information about hostels in Germany, contact the German Youth Hostel Association (*Deutsches Jugendherbergswerk – DJH*), Bülowstrasse 26, D-32756 Detmold. The following hostels are located in and around Munich:

DJH München, Wendl-Dietrich-Strasse 20, 80634 München, tel. 13 11 56.

DJH Jugendgästehaus München, Miesingstrasse 4, tel. 723 65 50.

DJH Burg Schwaneck, Burgweg 4-6, D-82049 Pullach, tel. 793 06 43.

Index

Where there is more than one set of references, the one in **bold** refers to the main entry, the one in *italic* to a photograph.